PALMARÈS

*P*ALMARÈS

By
RAYMOND GREENLAW

ROXY PUBLISHING, LLC
SAVANNAH, GEORGIA
UNITED STATES OF AMERICA

COPY EDITOR—Marjorie Roxburgh
COVER DESIGN—Robert Greenlaw, Jr.
TEXT DESIGN—Raymond Greenlaw
PHOTOGRAPHER—Shigeki Makino
TYPESETTING—Raymond Greenlaw

ROXY PUBLISHING, LLC
Savannah, Georgia 31419
United States of America

http://drraymondgreenlaw.com
First edition, paperback.

ISBN 978-1-947467-22-4 (Paperback)

Dedication

To the greatest athletes in the world,
Thanks for your inspirations.

Table of Contents

Preface

Palmarès is a French word meaning *a personal record of achievements*. It's a list. At the age of 27, once my formal studies were complete, I took up amateur sport seriously, focusing on activities that enhanced my life. This book presents my palmarès over a 30+ year period. These activities undertaken worldwide led me on a journey of self-discovery and a discovery of other lands, peoples, and cultures.

I hope this list (or your list) becomes more than a list to you; mine has to me. It represents a commitment to opening up to new challenges, to solving difficult problems, to confronting and overcoming fears, and to living an adventurous, healthy, and fulfilling life. This lifestyle meant creating and following dreams. I know there's always something waiting around the next corner. Challenges have been a compass, pointing me in the direction of life's path, while providing camaraderie, entertainment, and purpose.

Each chapter begins with a quote from me. Some have been modified from something that I heard or read along the way. In a few cases I'm not claiming 100% originality, but I don't have any sources to cite. My website is drraymondgreenlaw.com. I reference it several times in the body of this book.

Although I tried to be as careful as possible in my writing, a few grammatical errors and typos may remain. I apologize in advance. I would like to eliminate any errors in future editions of this work. I appreciate any corrections.

Raymond Greenlaw
October 10, 2021

Acknowledgments

A special thanks to Wongduean "Kig" Bohthong for her support and encouragement.

Thanks to Marjorie Roxburgh for her careful reading and comments on the manuscript.

Thanks to my nephew Robert Greenlaw, Jr. for designing the cover.

Thanks to my best friends Geir Agnarsson, Theresa Araneta, Glenn "Fiddlehead" Fleagle, Paul "Tarman" Göransson, Barry Fussell, Sanpawat "Bobby" Kantabutra, Shigeki "Shagg" Makino, Patrick Messer, Mirna Morrison, Andrew "Huck Lem" Phillips, Adrian "Aceman" Plante, Marjorie Roxburgh, Peter "Fish out of Water" Solomon, Linda Spring-Andrews, James "Jimbo" Wogulis, and Nuj Wongprapas for sharing and proposing many adventures over the years. Thanks for opening my eyes wider than I could have ever done without you. Sincere apologies to anyone whom I accidentally omitted.

Thanks to my other friends, colleagues, training partners, and students who helped make everything special and worthwhile. Sharing our good times has been very meaningful to my life. Thanks to my competitors, fellow hikers and divers, and companions. Having you by my side or knowing you were out there preparing enhanced my journey.

A sincere thanks to reviewers and early readers who provided me with constructive comments. Your suggestions helped to improve this book. I'm indebted to you. Many others contributed to this project, and a warm thanks goes out to each of you.

1. Introduction

"Keep working away at it."

Palmarès is a French word meaning *a personal record of achievements*. It's a list. At the age of 27, once my formal studies were complete, I took up amateur sport seriously, focusing on activities that enhanced my life. This book presents my palmarès over a 30+ year period. These activities undertaken worldwide led me on a journey of self-discovery and a discovery of other lands, peoples, and cultures.

I hope this list (or your list) becomes more than a list to you; mine has to me. It represents a commitment to opening up to new challenges, to solving difficult problems, to confronting and overcoming fears, and to living an adventurous, healthy, and fulfilling life. This lifestyle meant creating and following dreams. I know there's always something waiting around the next corner. Challenges have been a compass, pointing me in the direction of life's path, while providing camaraderie, entertainment, and purpose.

My interest in sports began at a young age. My brother Rob is an exceptional athlete. After watching Dave Wottle win the 800 meters at the Munich Olympics in 1972, Rob took up track and field (referred to as *athletics* in most parts of the world). I saw that race too. I was 11. I watch reruns. Dave lagged so far behind his competitors that the commentators surmised he was injured. His come-from-behind victory never fails to raise goosebumps. He wore a baseball cap—a regular guy from next door. Dave shook hands with opponents. He apologized to the American people for forgetting to remove his trademark cap during the playing of The Star-Spangled Banner. His down-to-earth friendly nature make him a likable character. Dave provides inspiration.

My parents played tennis. My best friend growing up, Peter "Fish out of Water" Solomon or Fish for short, was a world-class swimmer. He set swimming records in backstroke that stood for 50 years, until they changed the flip-turn rules. A boy in the neighborhood named Bruce Fischer was one of the greatest sub-four-minute milers of his generation, racing against legends such as Marty Liquori and Steve Prefontaine. His brother Andy held the US high-school steeplechase record for over 40 years. Rob trained with Andy. My Riverside, Rhode Island neighborhood contained a surprising number of impressive athletes. I didn't realize they were some of the all-time bests.

My favorite sport growing up was basketball. I practiced hours per day. I counted how many shots I made: 561/778, miss, 561/779, hit, 562/780, … I put up 1,000 shots, reset the counter, and began again. The Providence College Friars inspired me. In 1973 they were one of the greatest college-hoop teams of all-time. If Marvin Barnes hadn't gotten injured against the Memphis State Tigers in the Final Four, Dave Gavitt's team with Ernie "No D" DiGregorio and Kevin "Take 'em, Make 'em" Stacom would have challenged *the* greatest men's college-basketball team in history for the NCAA title. John Wooden coached Bill Walton and the UCLA Bruins to a record 88 straight wins. On January 19, 1974, I watched Notre Dame score the last 12 points to beat the legendary Bruins, 71-70. I never forgot that loss, or win. I was 12. I cried. I smiled. I shook my head.

At that time I joined a Catholic Youth Organization in order to play basketball. Our team went 32-0. The Providence College Friars and Boston Celtics inspired us. With one second remaining in the championship game, while going up for a jumper to tie the score, I was fouled. The opposition called time-out to ice the shooter, me, a 12-year old. I wiped my hands on my socks. I dribbled a few times. I took a deep breath. I concentrated. I aimed for the back of the rim. I sank the first shot. They called a second time-out. We were down by one. My palms were sweaty. I followed my routine. I swished the second shot. My teammates mobbed me. We jumped up and down. Under pressure, I kept our dream alive. My practice paid off. We lost by five points in overtime though. Everyone cried. The streak ended just as UCLA's had. I hung my head. I walked home and practiced more.

As a youngster, I played on teams for street hockey, tennis, football, basketball, and swimming. I ran 20-mile walkathons. In high school I competed in cross-country, indoor track, tennis, and outdoor track. I lettered in four sports. I played golf and softball. I canoed and fished in the summer. I skated in the winter. When I attended Pomona College in the Los Angeles area, a track coach saw me throwing the javelin. He asked me to join the team. I did and scored a few points to help win a conference championship, but my focus was on my studies. The coach compared me to our college's record holder and national champion. I explained that my studies came first. My coach meant well. World-class throwers came to train with him.

While attending graduate school in Seattle at the University of Washington, I joined the Ski Club. I skied downhill and cross-country. I joined the Outdoor Club. I snowshoed. I climbed mountains. I continued running. A childhood friend named Claire Sullivan told me about ultra-marathons. Her friend Kim Moody set the world's second-fastest time for 50 miles. Claire ran in the Olympic-marathon trails. We trained together. My roommate's girlfriend Susan attended Bowdoin College with Joan Benoit Samuelson—the first gold medalist in the women's Olympic marathon and former world-record holder. Susan shared inspirational stories about Joanie's training runs.

I learned about the developing sport of triathlon. I admired the big four: Dave "The Man" Scott, Scott "ST" Tinley, Mark "The Grip" Allen, and Scott "The Terminator" Molina. I started combining my swimming, cycling, and running workouts. My graduate-school friend Doug Wiebe got me into riding centuries—100 miles on a bicycle. I rode one century for a fund raiser for Cheryl Marek who planned to ride RAAM—the unfathomable Race across America. I hiked in the mountains of the Pacific Northwest. I ventured onto the Pacific Crest Trail (PCT). I camped out. I met other backpackers.

After completing graduate school, I moved to New Hampshire. I lived near Lynn Jennings—a former world-record holder in the indoor 5,000 meters, a nine-time US cross-country champion, a three-time world cross-country champion, and a bronze medalist in the Barcelona

Olympics. Cathy O'Brien—a former world-record holder in the 10-mile run, a distinguished Olympian, and one of the best marathon runners in US history—also lived nearby. I saw Lynn and Cathy out running and bumped into them in Durham. Training partners of mine in New Hampshire were close friends with Joanie. I met and competed against her. I lost.

When I ran in the White Mountains, I met hikers who were completing the Appalachian Trail (AT). They talked about their experiences. I listened. I shook my head. Their stories and achievements inspired me. My best friend Paul "Tarman" Göransson and I began training together. We hiked. We ran marathons and ultra-marathons. I introduced him to Ironman triathlons. We swam and biked.

I heard of the Seven Summits through a fellow Pomona College alumni Frank Wells, who along with Dick Bass, attempted to become the first to climb them. Dick succeeded, while Frank never summited Mount Everest. Tarman and I started climbing the Seven Summits. My love for the sea came from watching Jacques Cousteau. When Tarman suggested I become a certified diver, I traveled to Turks and Caicos to complete my Open Water Certification. Tarman and I traveled all over the world to dive and climb. We said: "Get high and go low." Due to nitrogen buildup in the bloodstream while diving and reduced air pressure at altitude, these activities can't be done in the reverse order, without taking a break in between.

My love for travel sparked competing and hiking in faraway places. My friend Glenn "Fiddlehead" Fleagle, whom I met while thru-hiking the AT, relayed enticing stories about the PCT. He mentioned the triple-crown of hiking, involving the AT, PCT, and Continental Divide Trail (CDT). I decided to thru-hike the PCT and CDT, too. I became a Triple Crowner. Fiddlehead and I went to the Balkans to hike a long-distance trail. We sought out new trails together. We hiked in Thailand. As like-minded people shared their dreams and experiences with me, my bucket list grew.

I gained inspiration from other athletes. I admired their commitment, abilities, and struggles. I admired what they were doing. I enjoy the process of preparing for an activity, building confidence, achieving long-term gratification, and trying new things. I like adventure. When

I learned about someone's achievement, I subconsciously filed the thought away. Later, when an opportunity presented itself, those memories came flooding back, and I attempted to follow in the footsteps of my heroes.

Certain things I saw influenced my choices. Shortly after watching Cathy and Lynn competing at the Barcelona Olympics, I moved there for a year. I raced the Olympic-marathon course and finished in the Olympic stadium. I traveled to 36 of the 43 cities to host either the summer or winter Olympics. I ran on the track in most Olympic stadiums. While completing my laps, I became emotional. I envisioned myself running against great champions. Sometimes I won and other times I lost. My imagination fueled and continues to fuel my interest in sports.

When I see a great performance, I get inspired. Fish introduced me to competitive swimming. Cheryl Marek taught me about RAAM. After I met an experienced sky diver, I took a few jumps. My friend John Bates started me rock climbing. For each activity I took up, there was an inspiring person leading the way. In many cases I never met the person. I admired and piggybacked on others' achievements. Role models expanded my horizons. I gained confidence and formulated my own adventures. I branched out.

In hindsight a number of factors led me to my expanding palmarès. I possess a high-energy level. My close friends have a thirst for life, enjoy adventure, aren't afraid to fail, and are willing to commit time and resources to achieving long-term goals. I accepted encouragement from others and rejected naysayers. I visualized myself fulfilling my dreams. When I had an urge to participate, I followed it. I developed discipline and set goals, but I also learned to smell the roses. I love to train and see the benefits of hard work. I have many interests, and when opportunities arose, I took them. I rarely said no. I lived my dreams.

For the majority of my life, I haven't owned a TV. I prefer going outdoors and being active, as opposed to sitting indoors. Although I took risks and almost died on a number of occasions, I was fortunate not to sustain many serious injuries or broken bones. I appreciate and maintain my health. I learned what my body can and can't do. I eat a healthy diet. Although I received little formal coaching, I learned from listening to others and by observing how they achieved success. I possess a great curiosity about the world and myself. I enjoy pushing my limits. All these ingredients mixed together resulted in me completing a diverse range of activities, which I collected here in my palmarès.

Let me say a few words about how the remainder of this book is organized. In each chapter I list the items on my palmarès in chronological order. I provide the name of the event or activity, the date, times and split times (where relevant), my placing (when relevant), my age at the time, and other pertinent information. In most cases I provide an anecdote or elaborate on the item being described. The level of detail that I remember varies for different events. In some cases I provide an estimate or guess about a forgotten point if my research was inconclusive. Not all items are of equal significance or difficultly. They vary widely in terms of duration, cost, risk, preparation, skills, fitness, and planning required.

You may not want to read every detail in every entry. I hope you find the anecdotes interesting. The commitment, travel, recovery, and logistics involved in completing the more arduous events was substantial. Over the many disciplines and period discussed, a significant effort went into my activities. My natural journey led to the evolution of my palmarès. I never focused on building it. I trained far more than I competed. For example, I once rode my bicycle 40,000+ kilometers (24,800+ miles) in a year. I was shocked to learn that even during his prime, I trained more than the great four-time Tour de France champion Chris Froome.

I saved money from my professorship and spent it on equipment, training trips, entry fees, and travel. After suffering injuries, I required time to heal. As I aged, I became one of the oldest competitors in some of my events. I was born in 1961. I'm writing this at age 60. I'm not a professional athlete. I was an ordinary kid, who grew up in a middle-class family in Riverside, Rhode Island. While completing most of my activities, I worked a full-time job. I paid for everything. I never sought sponsors. My friends and I organized these trips. We rarely had support staff.

I hope you're able to take inspiration from my activities and formulate new dreams. Putting together my palmarès has helped me to see what's possible. Reviewing it lets me know what I'm missing. Just as every pro cyclist wants to add the Tour de France to their palmarès, I would like to ride the Tour's route and add it to mine. There are more things remaining than I have time to do. That realization motivates me to stay busy. As the COVID-19 pandemic proved, second chances may never present themselves.

There are many events/activities that I was involved with earlier in my life. However, I only started maintaining a palmarès in my late 20s. Although some early activities had a duration of a week, most were local, one-day events. They would triple the number of entries in my palmarès. With this background, let's dive into my palmarès. I divided things up according to activity type. In the next chapter I start off with hiking.

2. Hiking

"I just completed the Triple Crown."

I always enjoy walking in a forest, through the mountains, alongside a river, or on a seashore. I even enjoy walking around town. I haven't owned a vehicle for many years. Here I list my hikes longer than 700 miles. I took countless day hikes all over the world, and many shorter backpacking/day trips, especially in the states where I lived: Rhode Island, California, Washington, New Hampshire, Georgia, and Maryland. These states border 17 others and two countries. I had easy access to 23 states, Mexico, and Canada. As you'll see is often the case, I jumped in with both feet.

1. Appalachian Trail (AT):
    East Coast Mountains, USA

    Distance: 2,169 miles
    Dates: May 11 to August 16, 1995 (97 days)
    My age: 34

    Notes: I hiked the AT with Fish. We flew to Atlanta together. For many years I ran trails along the AT in Maine, Vermont, and New Hampshire. While living in New Hampshire, each fall season in spectacular New England foliage, I met northbound thru-hikers on their way to the northern terminus of the AT—the majestic Mount Katahdin. They had a certain glint in their eyes. They were hungry. Other than sore feet, stress levels were down, and they seemed genuinely happy. They would be finishing their thru-hikes soon.

The northbound hikers whom I met seemed fulfilled, and most were in great shape. They possessed a sense of achievement and exuded confidence. Some hikers said: "Once you complete the AT, you can do anything." Many believe this statement to be true. The hikers who weren't enjoying their hikes dropped out before reaching Vermont. My hiker conversations reached a tipping point, where I wanted to do what the thru-hikers were doing and get that glint in my eyes. My typical nine-month contract allowed me 90 days off during the summer. In this case I stretched it to 100.

The southbound thru-hikers whom I met in late spring and early summer didn't convince me to hike the AT. They were in rough shape from hiking through a swampy Maine, starting out with too heavy a pack, enduring terrible biting flies and mosquitoes, and lacking the fitness for the steep, rocky climbs. I guess most of those folks didn't make it to Springer Mountain. I'm sure the successful hikers who were entering Georgia, while hiking from Maine, possessed a wonderful glint in their eyes.

Fish and I went northbound. We reached an important milestone after a few weeks, when we threw away our return airplane tickets to save weight. Back then, it was cheaper to purchase a round-trip fare. Shredding those tickets showed commitment and confidence. A few weeks later I sustained a serious ankle injury. I took a number of rest days, and Fish reluctantly forged ahead. With trepidation, I started hiking again. I pushed through my pain and hiked the remainder of the trail solo.

I hiked the trail pure, meaning that I covered the entire white-blazed, designated AT without deviation. This meant if I got lost and missed a section of trail, I returned to where I unintentionally had deviated. I took seven rest days, mostly related to my bad ankle. Fish completed his thru-hike as well. Although my injury forced us to split up, we both found ways to see our dreams through to the end. That ability to adapt helped me to complete many activities on my palmarès. After our thru-hikes, Fish and I celebrated our successes and share trail stories. Whenever we meet, we reminisce about the good old days on the AT. We don't talk about the hardships or my injury. Unfavorable memories dissipate more quickly than pleasant ones.

My biggest day on the AT was 45 miles. On hiking days I averaged 24.1. In memory of my hike on a sidewalk in the small town of Damascus, Virginia, there's a decorated brick with my trail-name Wall painted on it. During my bicycle ride of the Trans America Trail, I visited my brick. Fond memories came flooding back. The brick empowered me for the remainder of my ride across America.

2. Pacific Crest Trail (PCT):
   West Coast Mountains, USA

Distance: 2,659 miles
Dates: May 12 to August 2, 2003 (83 days)
My age: 41

Notes: Due to work constraints, I drew up an ambitious schedule to hike the PCT in 88 days. I ran my draft by Fiddlehead because he's an expert on the PCT. My schedule was two days shy of the world record for the fastest hike of the PCT (the Fastest Known Time, FKT), so Fiddlehead suggested that I try and set the FKT. I sat down with my Excel spreadsheet again. In 45 minutes I trimmed three days.

I ended up setting the FKT by an additional two days. Most of the time I walked alone. I went northbound. I hiked the trail pure without any navigational aids. Fish joined me for about ten days in California, and Tarman hiked with me for the final week in Washington State. He was inspired. While I'm writing this, Tarman at age 67 is finishing up his section hike of the PCT. He also thru-hiked the AT.

My book *The Pacific Crest Trail: Its Fastest Hike* describes my hike. Setting the FKT for the PCT required a great commitment and a huge physical effort. I took risks. My record has long since been broken. Conditions have changed. The PCT has become a popular trail. Many hikers rely on software applications (such as Guthook Guides) and GPS units. This makes hiking safer and simpler. When I hiked the trail, such tools weren't available. Fiddlehead told me: "Just follow footsteps in the sand." We laugh about that now, but in the deserts of California, I wasn't laughing.

My biggest day was 48 miles. My biggest week was 325 miles. I averaged 32+ miles of trail per day. I often needed to walk long distances off trail and back for resupplies. I got lost many times, as the trail wasn't as well marked or worn, as it is now. The PCT taught me many lessons. It was far more remote and much higher than the AT.

3. Continental Divide Trail (CDT):
Continental Divide, USA

Distance: 2,800 miles
Dates: April 25 to August 2, 2015 (100 days)
My age: 54

Notes: I went northbound from the Mexican border, following the Ley Route. My friend Shigeki "Shagg" Makino hiked with me for the first week. We only saw a couple of other hikers. After Shagg departed, I continued alone. I missed him. When I arrived near the Colorado border, due to avalanche danger and flooding, many sections of the CDT were closed. I learned about which ones from Fish. After attempting to push north of the New Mexico-Colorado border, groups of strong hikers were forced to retreat. I altered my plans.

I drove north to South Pass City, Wyoming. I walked south for two weeks across the windy Great Basin. Then I drove back to the point where I'd left off near Chama, New Mexico. Due to trail closures and high snow levels, I did a lot of road walking in Colorado. When I reached the Colorado-Wyoming border again, because eight feet of snow had melted, I didn't recognize the area. From there I drove past the southern Wyoming section that I'd hiked already. From where I'd gone south at South Pass City a month earlier, I went north toward the border with Canada.

Because other thru-hikers traveled to the US-Canadian border from the New Mexico-Colorado border to avoid the Colorado snow, I went weeks without seeing anybody. I was probably the only thru-hiker that year who went north for the majority of the trail. Once halfway into Montana, I began encountering old friends. They were hiking south. We greeted each other by trail name but with some uncertainty, as our appearances and dispositions had changed significantly in a matter of weeks. We shared stories and helpful information. I walked around several large fires in Montana.

For the most part, I followed the Bear Creek Route, except where there were trail closures. I relied on road-atlas maps, the Ley maps, the Guthook Guides, Yogi's book, and my GPS. On many days, I didn't encounter any hikers. My friend Marjorie Roxburgh sent me a handful of mail drops. Whenever I received a package, it was very meaningful. I completed a northbound walk, except for the two weeks where I went south. The entire route was an uninterrupted, continuous, border-to-border hike.

Completing the CDT meant finishing the Triple Crown of hiking. At that time less than 200 hikers claimed to be Triple Crowners. The trail itself was cold, hot, high, snowy, dry, remote, poorly marked, beautiful, difficult, peaceful, full of wildlife, and spectacular. The CDT taught me many lessons. It was more difficult than the AT or PCT. I would love to hike the CDT again. It stimulates personal growth. It's by far my favorite trail, as Fiddlehead had told me it would be.

My biggest day was 40 miles. I averaged 28 miles per day. I think of the CDT daily.

4. Via Dinarica White Trail (VDWT):
    Slovenia to Albania

    Distance: 780 miles
    Dates: July 4 to August 24, 2017 (52 days)

My age: 56

Notes: Fiddlehead and I completed one of the first thru-hikes of the GPS route for this (at the time) new trail through Slovenia, Croatia, Bosnia-Herzegovina, Montenegro, and Albania. There were many places where it appeared as if no one had ever hiked the route, even though we were on a published GPS track. The route seemed designed by someone sitting in an office. We were lost frequently and bushwhacked through exceptionally rugged terrain, where there was no trail. When frustrated, we said: "The Via Dinarica, it's not for everybody."

We hiked past mine fields. When bushwhacking, we would say: "You go first." Back came: "Naw, you go ahead." The challenges of being on foreign soil, being unable to speak Russian and local languages, and crossing borders in places without official crossings made this hike a rewarding adventure. The route has since been extended, hopefully via a real trail. I'm sure this beautiful trail will develop and become better marked over time. Through our blogging, documentation, and discussions with others, I hope we made it easier and safer to complete the trail.

Our hike was prior to the route being extended into Kosovo. We hiked in the middle of summer. Finding water is a serious problem in the karst. We relied on cisterns. As the trail develops, I hope the cisterns are made available to hikers and marked. Our biggest day was 25 miles. I got terribly sick with vomiting and diarrhea. We took several rest days. On hiking days, we averaged 20 miles.

5. <u>East to West Walk across Thailand:</u>
    Ubon Ratchathani, Thailand/Laos border to Mae Hong Son, Thailand/Myanmar border

    Distance: 725 miles
    Dates: March 12 to April 3, 2018 (22 days and 9 hours)
    My age: 56

Notes: Starting at the PK Riverside Resort, Ubon Ratchathani, I hiked alone from the easternmost point of the mainland of Thailand to its westernmost point, reaching the Salawin River View Point at Mae Sam Laep, Mae Hong Son. My hike got off to a rough start, as I suffered from terrible blisters. They plagued me throughout. I completed a hot walk, meaning my hike was done during the hottest months in Thailand. I was supported by Wongduean "Kig" Bohthong and her eight-year old daughter Jennie, aka Princess. I only carried snacks and water.

The challenges of this hike are heat and humidity, dogs, snakes, insects, traffic, and pollution. My shoes melted. I bought some at a store in the middle-of-nowhere. The selection for size 12 is limited. The hike is detailed in my book *The Fastest Hike across Thailand*. My biggest day was 37 miles. I averaged 32.4 miles—identical to my PCT mileage from 15 years earlier.

Naturally, without preparation and training, one doesn't just hop onto the longest trails in the world. Those adventurous spirits who do usually fail, and sadly sometimes don't live to share their stories. They don't average 25+ miles per day. Just as in life, everyone needs to follow their own path at their own speed. I put in hundreds of shorter hikes. They helped prepare me for my longer ones. I participated in many mountaineering expeditions. When the going got tough, as it sometimes did on my longer hikes, I had the experience to help me work through issues.

Hiking connects me with nature, helps me develop spiritually, brings me new friends, tests my will power, gets me into great shape, generates crazy adventures, gives me time to reflect, lets me eat huge quantities of food, and provides me with memorable experiences. As any thru-hiker can attest, hiking presents challenges and dangers. I was struck by lightning on the AT, crossed weak snow bridges and forded swollen rivers on the PCT, walked past a momma grizzly bear with her cubs on the CDT, crossed through mined areas in the Balkans on the VDWT, ran out of food, and battled absurd heat and humidity in Thailand. The rewards outweighed the risks. I plan to continue hiking and seeking out the world's longest trails.

3. Cycling Rides

"Yeah, I'm tired."

As a child, I learned to ride a bicycle. I grew up in a neighborhood in Rhode Island, where it's safe to ride. When I was 13 years old, I paid a visit to my grandmother's house. She lived 30 miles away. I asked her if it would be okay if my friend John "Spooky" Allen and I rode over sometime. Although Mémé thought I was joking, Spooky and I completed the ride the very next day. My Mémé was shocked. After a good night's sleep, we rode back home.

I completed my first one-day, 200-mile ride with Fish at age 15. We cycled from Riverside, Rhode Island to Provincetown, Massachusetts, and back to Onset. While attending Pomona College in Southern California, I rode in outstanding weather: both for enjoyment and general transportation. I rode to the Ice Station on Mount Baldy, Huntington Beach and back, and to Lake Big Bear. My friend Grant "Minnow" Mason and I rode from San Francisco down the Pacific Coast Highway to the LA area. While attending graduate school at the University of Washington in Seattle, I cycled in the windy, rainy Pacific Northwest. My friend Doug Wiebe and I rode many centuries together. When I took up the Ironman triathlon, I increased my riding volume.

When I lived in New Hampshire, Georgia, and Maryland, I continued as an avid cyclist. But, when I relocated to Thailand for part of each year, I started riding more and farther, much farther. During my biggest training year, I covered the distance around the Earth: 24,800+ miles. I love riding in the big, steep, remote mountains. My book *The Hazards of Cycling in Thailand* discusses the dangers of riding in The Land of Smiles. The heat and humidity there challenge all long-distance riders.

I discovered quiet routes throughout Thailand. I found steep, paved roads with gradients up to 28%. As my rides became one- to two-week solo forays, the Race across America (RAAM) entered my consciousness again. I remembered the fund raiser to support Cheryl Marek's RAAM ride. In preparation for RAAM, I increased my training volume further. I remember the head of the RAAM organization Fred Boethling saying to me: "Don't underestimate the difficulty of RAAM." I took Fred's admonishment seriously.

With this background, let me review a few facts about my cycling. I start out by presenting the number of times that I rode various distances or farther within 24 hours:

- 100 miles: 1,160
- 200 miles: 57
- 300 miles: 12
- 350 miles: 7

Note, for example, that's a century or farther every day for 3.4 years, one a week for 24.3 years, and one every other week for 48.6 years. I estimate that one third of my century rides exceeded 150 miles and about 20% of them were 175+ miles, but less than 200. This means I rode 175+ miles in a day 300+ times. During the COVID-19 lockdown, I learned that the majority of the men's pro peloton had *never* ridden this far in a single day. Because races were postponed, some pro riders did longer training rides in 2020. People on social media gushed over such "long" rides.

I next list my cycling trips longer than 500 miles. Note that races aren't included in this list. They're described in the next chapter. As time went on and I acquired a GPS, I kept better track of my routes and climbing data. When available, I provide enough details so that another rider can retrace my route. For those not familiar with some areas, while reading through route descriptions, it may help to trace my route on a map. Descriptions of well-established routes (for example, RAAM and TAT) can be found on the Internet. For each entry, when available, I provide the dates, my age, distance, bicycle type, time, my partner (if not riding solo), and notes. Notes consist of general comments, route descriptions, or tidbits that readers might find interesting. My book *Raymond's Checklist Cycling Gear* provides additional information, for example, about where I stayed, my bike packs, what I was carrying, and how much things weighed.

1. Crossing the USA:
   Provincetown, Massachusetts to San Diego, California

   Dates: April 28 to June 4, 2011
   My age: 49
   Distance: 3,477 miles
   Bicycle: Trek Madone 5.5, road bike
   Time: 36 days
   Partner: Peter Solomon

   Notes: I rode unsupported from Provincetown, Massachusetts to San Diego, California with Fish. On our east to west crossing of the continent, we joined the RAAM route in northern Maryland. We found out that reading directions in reverse doesn't always work, that the early versions of Google's biking directions contained many errors, that it was easiest to get lost in our little home state of Rhode Island, and that some people in Connecticut don't know the name of the street where they live. We maintained a blog, and it's linked from my website.

   Before we left Provincetown, I let Adrian "Aceman" Plante know that we would be arriving at his place in San Diego at 3:00 PM on June 4. When we showed up at 3:30 PM on the designated day, he quipped: "You're half an hour late." We laughed ourselves silly. Due to road closures and a terrible sand storm in Arizona, we rode about 35 miles of the trip from west to east. We needed to hitch-hike forward at the end of one day. Then we rode back to where we hitch-hiked from, and due to horrendous blowing sand, after some discussion, we hitch-hiked back to where we'd started that day. We deviated from the RAAM route in Southern California because our destination was San Diego not Oceanside. There were no gaps in our route. Fish and I often chatted about the AT. We averaged just under 100 miles per day for our first ride over 3,000 miles.

2. Euro Velo 6:
   Budapest, Hungary to Constanta, Romania

   Dates: May 23 to June 5, 2012
   My age: 50
   Distance: 680 miles (approximate)
   Bicycle: Hungarian model, hybrid bike
   Time: 13 days
   Partner: Paul Göransson

   Notes: Tarman and I purchased new, hybrid bicycles in Budapest. I corresponded with a guy there named George. When we finally found George's bicycle shop in Budapest, we spoke to a petite, young woman. I asked her if George was around. She informed me she's George. We smiled. She helped us get the bikes setup and took care of all our needs.

   Tarman and I rode unsupported through Hungary, Croatia, Serbia, Bulgaria, and Romania. The bikes held up well. The only mechanical problem was breaking a kickstand. At the end of our ride, we sold the bicycles in Constanta. Although we lost money, the amount was far less than the $800 that we would have paid for shipping bicycles. It's much simpler to fly without a bicycle. We maintained a blog, and it's linked from my website. We averaged 50 miles per day and one beer every 10 miles.

3. Chiang Mai to Phuket Return:
   Chiang Mai to Phuket, Thailand

   Dates: April 14 to April 23, 2013
   My age: 51
   Distance: 2,010 miles
   Bicycle: Specialized S-Works Roubaix, road bike

Time: 9 days and 11 hours

Partner: solo

Notes: This unsupported ride was part of my RAAM training. I traveled far west of Bangkok through Kanchanaburi—the place where the Bridge over the River Kwai is located. I reversed my route on the way back. April is the hottest month in Thailand with a heat index often 120°+F. I learned that riding during the Songkran water festival is the most dangerous time to ride in Thailand. Many people drink and drive. I saw many bad accidents.

I got water thrown on me constantly. Although the cooling effect was nice, having buckets of water thrown in your face about 1,000 times per day is disconcerting. The buckets sometimes contain ice cubes. Even though I did some to meet my intended mileages, I don't recommend night riding in Thailand. I averaged 210+ miles per day.

4. Chiang Mai to Bueng Gan Return:
   Chiang Mai to Bueng Gan, Thailand

Dates: May 5 to May 11, 2013

My age: 52

Distance: 1,044 miles

Bicycle: Specialized S-Works Roubaix, road bike

Time: 5 days and 10 hours

Partner: solo

Notes: I rode unsupported. I consulted a map to determine my route. It was entirely new to me. I decided to go Chiang Mai, Lamphun, Lampang, Phrae, Uttaradit, Phitsanulok, Loei, Nong Bua Lamphu, Udon Thani, Nong Khai, and Bueng Gan. I reversed my course on the way back. I especially enjoyed riding along the border with Laos—in the mountains and along the Mekong River. Once it became dark, usually before 7:00 PM, many dogs pursued me. One night I slept in a spare room (cell) at a police station. The insects prevented me from sleeping outdoors. Having no idea what to expect in terms of accommodations, resupply, and terrain, my first east-west ride across Thailand was a true adventure. I averaged 190+ miles per day.

5. Chiang Mai to Bueng Gan Return:
Chiang Mai to Bueng Gan, Thailand

Dates: Winter 2014
My age: 52
Distance: 1,051 miles
Bicycle: Specialized S-Works Roubaix, road bike
Time: 7 days
Partner: solo

Notes: I rode unsupported via Chiang Mai, Lamphun, Lampang, Phrae, Nan, Uttaradit, Phitsanulok, Loei, Nong Khai, and Bueng Gan. I reversed my course on the way back. While crossing Thailand this time, I cycled through Nan province. I call this the *hard mountainous route*, as there are many steep climbs in Nan and down through Uttaradit and Phitsanulok, especially along the Laotian border. I averaged 150 miles per day.

6. Chiang Mai to Phuket Partial Return:
Chiang Mai to Phuket, Thailand

Dates: Spring 2014
My age: 52
Distance: 1,400 miles
Bicycle: Specialized S-Works Roubaix, road bike
Time: 9 days
Partner: solo

Notes: I traveled far west of Bangkok through Kanchanaburi. I reversed my course on the way back, until I stopped for sightseeing. Kig provided direct support near Phuket. I averaged 156 miles per day.

7. Chiang Mai to Bueng Gan Return:
Chiang Mai to Bueng Gan, Thailand

Dates: Fall 2014
My age: 53
Distance: 1,048 miles
Bicycle: Specialized S-Works Roubaix, road bike
Time: 7 days
Partner: solo

Notes: I rode unsupported via the hard mountainous route across northern Thailand. I averaged 150 miles per day.

8. Chiang Mai to Phuket Partial Return:
Chiang Mai to Phuket, Thailand

Dates: Spring 2015
My age: 53
Distance: 1,200 miles
Bicycle: Specialized S-Works Roubaix, road bike
Time: 10 days
Partner: solo

Notes: I traveled far west of Bangkok through Kanchanaburi. Kig provided support. We did some sightseeing. I averaged 120 miles per day.

9. Chiang Mai to Bueng Gan Return:
Chiang Mai to Bueng Gan, Thailand

Dates: Fall 2015
My age: 54
Distance: 1,140 miles
Bicycle: Specialized S-Works Roubaix, road bike
Time: 8 days

Partner: solo

Notes: Kig supported me on the hard mountainous route across northern Thailand. I rode during rainy season. Even when dry, the descents are scary. I wish the Roubaix had disc brakes. I averaged 143 miles per day.

10. Chiang Mai to Bueng Gan Return:
    Chiang Mai to Bueng Gan, Thailand

    Dates: Winter 2016
    My age: 54
    Distance: 1,044 miles
    Bicycle: Specialized S-Works Roubaix, road bike
    Time: 9 days
    Partner: solo

    Notes: I rode unsupported via the hard mountainous route across northern Thailand. Winter is the best time to ride in Thailand. I averaged 116 miles per day.

11. Chiang Mai to Bueng Gan Return:
    Chiang Mai to Bueng Gan, Thailand

    Dates: Spring 2016
    My age: 54
    Distance: 1,133 miles
    Bicycle: Specialized S-Works Roubaix, road bike
    Time: 10 days
    Partner: solo

    Notes: Kig supported me on the hard mountainous route across northern Thailand. It's exceptionally hot in the spring months. I suffered in the heat. I averaged 113 miles per day.

12. Chiang Mai to Bueng Gan to Ubon Ratchathani Return:

Chiang Mai to Bueng Gan to Ubon Ratchathani to Chiang Mai, Thailand

Dates: Spring 2016
My age: 54
Distance: 1,426 miles
Bicycle: Specialized S-Works Roubaix, road bike
Time: 14 days
Partner: solo

Notes: I rode unsupported via Chiang Mai, Lamphun, Lampang, Phrae, Nan, Uttaradit, Phitsanulok, Loei, Nong Khai, Bueng Gan, Sakon Nakhon, Mukdahan, Amnat Charoen, Ubon Ratchathani, Si Saket, Surin, Buriram, Chaiyaphum, Phetchabun, Phitsanulok, Uttaradit, Phrae, Lampang, Lamphun, and Chiang Mai. I covered a lot of new territory, especially along the Thai-Cambodian border. The road surface was rough for the Roubaix. I averaged 100+ miles per day.

13. Chiang Mai to Bueng Gan Return:
    Chiang Mai to Bueng Gan, Thailand

Dates: Fall 2016
My age: 55
Distance: 1,027 miles
Bicycle: Specialized S-Works Roubaix, road bike
Time: 10 days
Partner: solo

Notes: Kig supported me on the hard mountainous route across northern Thailand. Each year additional gravel sections of the route have been paved. Since I first rode this route, many road improvements were made. Although harder on the Roubaix, I prefer the gravel sections. I prefer the area remaining natural. I averaged 100+ miles per day.

14. Chiang Mai to Hanoi:
Chiang Mai, Thailand to Hanoi, Vietnam

Dates: February 17 to March 6, 2017
My age: 55
Distance: 700 miles (approximate)
Bicycle: Specialized Epic Carbon, mountain bike
Time: 18 days
Partner: Paul Göransson

Notes: Tarman and I rode unsupported via Chiang Mai, Fang, Chiang Rai, Chiang Khong, Houay Xai, Pak Tha, Pak Beng, Xayaboury, Luang Prabang, Pak Mong, Muang Lai, Muang Mai, Dien Bien Phu, Tuan Giao, Muong Lay, Lai Chau, Phong Tho, a middle route across Vietnam, and Hanoi. The route involved long sections of dirt roads and was remote. It was hot, especially for Tarman, who arrived to Thailand from Maine.

At one point we squeezed past a jackknifed semi, which dangled over a precipice. For several days no vehicles passed us from behind. When word spread about the blocked road, few vehicles came toward us either. It was an adventure—finding and following the route mapped out online, securing accommodations, and obtaining supplies. We had limited mobile service. The guesthouses are beautiful in Laos.

In many villages smiling children ran alongside us. At all hours of the day, they shouted their only English phrase, clearly not understanding its meaning: "Good morning, teacher." We responded with: "Good X, class," where X represented morning, afternoon, or evening depending on the time of day. We encountered enormous Chinese construction vehicles being used to build dams in Laos. In order for these vehicles to travel through Laos, the Chinese widened and improved many roads. Such main roads had reasonable gradients and a smooth surface.

Tarman's rear tire suffered a gash. It took days to find a replacement. We moved his rear tire to the front, so he could avoid sharp rocks. When my pump failed, we bought one from a villager.

My Thai-language skills came in handy. In dense fog we rode up and down mountains, while avoiding livestock on the roads. The part labeled 'middle route across Vietnam' in my description is where we deviated from our intended route, after Tarman developed severe bronchitis. On riding days we averaged 50 miles.

15. Chiang Mai to Bueng Gan Return:
    Chiang Mai to Bueng Gan, Thailand

    Dates: Winter 2017
    My age: 55
    Distance: 1,041 miles
    Bicycle: Specialized Epic Carbon, mountain bike
    Time: 10 days
    Partner: solo

    Notes: Kig supported me on the hard mountainous route across northern Thailand. For the first time, I completed it on a mountain bike. The granny gear and disc brakes helped. The front suspension and wider tires made for a smoother ride, especially on gravel sections. I averaged 105 miles per day.

16. Chiang Mai to Bueng Gan Return:
    Chiang Mai to Bueng Gan, Thailand

    Dates: April 28 to May 8, 2017
    My age: 55
    Distance: 1,044 miles
    Bicycle: Specialized Epic Carbon, mountain bike
    Time: 10 days
    Partner: solo

    Notes: Kig supported me on the hard mountainous route across northern Thailand. It was extremely hot and humid. I averaged 105 miles per day in brutal conditions.

17. <u>Chiang Mai to Bueng Gan Return:</u>
Chiang Mai to Bueng Gan, Thailand

Dates: October 5 to October 10, 2017
My age: 56
Distance: 611 miles
Bicycle: Specialized Epic Carbon, mountain bike
Time: 6 days
Partner: solo

Notes: Kig supported me. I only completed a partial ride, as rainy season took its toll. I passed through Nakorn Thai on my way to Issarn—the northeast region of Thailand. I averaged 102 miles per day.

18. <u>Chiang Mai to Luang Prabang Return:</u>
Chiang Mai, Thailand to Luang Prabang, Laos

Dates: April 12 to April 22, 2018
My age: 56
Distance: 803 miles
Bicycle: Specialized Epic Carbon, mountain bike
Climbing: 42,147 feet
Time: 9 days of riding
Partner: solo

Notes: Kig supported me for most of the ride on a route via Chiang Mai, Lamphun, Lampang, Phrae, Den Chai, Uttaradit, Nam Pat, Pu Soi Dao (detour from Phuu Duu border), Pu Soi Dao, Tha Li, Xayaboury, Luang Prabang, Na Mor, Huay Xai, Chiang Khon, Chiang Rai, Fang, Chiang Dao, and Chiang Mai. Temperatures reached 108°F (42°C) on most days. Only Thais and Laotians can cross the border at Phuu Duu. We weren't aware of this fact. I completed a long detour to Tha Li to reach the next border crossing. In record-breaking heat, I averaged 90 miles and a vertical mile per day.

19. Chiang Mai to Vientiane to Lampang Partial Return: Chiang Mai, Thailand to Vientiane, Laos

Dates: April 28 to May 17, 2018
My age: 56
Distance: 1,370 miles
Bicycle: Specialized Epic Carbon, mountain bike
Climbing: 46,609 feet
Time: 16 days of riding
Partner: solo

Notes: Kig partially supported me on a route via Chiang Mai, Lamphun, Lampang, Long (Phrae), Den Chai (Phrae), Uttaradit, Chat Trakan (Phitsanulok), Nakhon Thai (Phitsanulok), Dansai (Loei), Tha Li (Loei), Kean Thao (Loei, border), Na Phor (Laos), Xayaboury, Nan City, Kasi, Hin Hoeup, Vang Vieng, Vientiane, Nong Khai, Bueng Gan, Si Chiang Mai (Nong Khai), Tha Li, Chat Trakan, Uttaradit, Phrae, and Lampang.

From Muang Nan to Kasi, there's an hors catégorie (meaning too hard to be categorized) climb of six miles at 14% average gradient. The road climbs to 6,000 feet. The area is considered dangerous because over the years, Hmong rebels have killed a number of tourists in the region. The descent is exceptionally dangerous, especially in wet conditions such as I experienced. Three semis remained vertically on end after crashing. Kig was shaking from *driving* down the descent. The descent worried me far more than the Hmong rebels.

Temperatures exceeded 104°F (40°C) on most days. The high was 110°F (43+°C) with humidity. The heat index topped 150°F. While descending a steep, switchbacked road one day, I felt something weird. Moments after stopping, my front tire blew out. I was lucky that didn't happen on the next hairpin bend. With giant, swarming insects biting, fixing a flat in such heat isn't easy.

There was a terrible lightning storm on the last day, so I picked up in Lampang. I didn't want to press my luck any further by riding over a mountain pass in a storm. On riding days I averaged 86 miles.

20. Trans America Trail (TAT):
Astoria, Oregon to Yorktown, Virginia

Dates: May 27 to July 8, 2018
My age: 56
Distance: 4,326 miles
Bicycle: Specialized Epic Carbon, mountain bike
Time: 42.5 days
Partner: 20 days with Andy Phillips, remainder solo

Notes: I didn't see another rider doing the TAT on a mountain bike. Although much heavier, the mountain bike is more comfortable and stable than a road bike. I only got two flats. We rode unsupported. We maintained a blog, and it's linked from my website. Many details are provided there.

I loved riding the TAT. I make mention of it again in the best experiences chapter. On my mountain bike, I averaged 102 miles per day for six weeks. I took no rest days. The longest day was 150 miles.

21. Chiang Mai around Northern Thailand Return:
Chiang Mai to Ubon Ratchathani to Nakhon Phanom to Chiang Mai, Thailand

Dates: November 4-28, 2018
My age: 57
Distance: 2,079 miles
Bicycle: Specialized Epic Carbon, mountain bike
Time: 19 days of riding
Partner: solo

Notes: Kig supported me for five days on a route via Chiang Mai, Lamphun, Lampang, Sukhothai, Phitsanulok, Phichit, Phetchabun,

Chaiyaphum, Nakhon Ratchasima, Buriram, Surin, Si Saket, Ubon Ratchathani, Amnat Charoen, Mukdahan, Nakhon Phanom, Bueng Gan, Nong Khai, Loei, Phitsanulok, Uttaradit, Nan, Phayao, Chiang Rai, and Chiang Mai. I covered new ground.

Near Cambodia I broke a rim. It caused six mysterious flats and a three-day delay. I acquired a new rim in Ubon Ratchathani, but to make a wheel, we needed to reuse my old spokes. November is usually dry, and one of the best months to ride in Thailand. I averaged 110 miles per day, which is a lot on a loaded mountain bike, especially with all those flats.

22. Chiang Mai around Northern Thailand Return:
Chiang Mai to 33 provinces, and return to Chiang Mai, Thailand

Dates: August 2 to October 19, 2020
My age: 59
Distance: 4,556 miles
Bicycle: Specialized Epic Carbon, mountain bike
Time: 58 days of riding
Partner: solo

Notes: During the COVID-19 pandemic, I completed this unsupported ride in rainy season. When my GPS got wet on day three, I lost my maps. I got two flats, 14 wasp/bee stings, two new chains, two new sets of brake pads, new clothes, and new tires. I climbed Phu Chi Fah nonstop via Route 4018 from Chiang Rai. I descended via Thoeng. That out-and-back ride was 127 miles (205K). The climb up Route 4018 is hors catégorie with long stretches well over 20%. I feared coming down Route 4018 without a dropper seat-post, which is why I rode a much longer route back via Thoeng.

I rode 26 centuries with a biggest day of 175 miles—a long way on a loaded mountain bike. I don't anticipate going that far again, unless there's an emergency. My route was via Chiang Mai, Lamphun, Lampang, Sawankhalok, Sukhothai, Phitsanulok, Wang Tong, Phetchabun, Lomsak, Chaiyaphum, Chum Pae, Khon Kaen,

Maha Sarakham, Kalasin, Sakon Nakhon, Nakhon Phanom, Ban Phaeng, Seka, So Phisai, Bueng Gan, Nong Khai, Udon Thani, Ban Phaeng, Nakhon Phanom, Mukdahan, Yasothon, Amnat Charoen, Ubon Ratchathani, Khong Chiam, Si Saket, Surin, Buriram, Prakhon Chai, Aranyaphrathet, Sa Kaeo, Chantaburi, Trat, Ban Hat Lek, Chantaburi, Soi Dao, Prachin Buri, Sa Kaeo, Cabin Buri, Chok Chai, Nakhon Ratchasima, Buriram, Maha Sarakham, Mancha Kiri, Khon Kaen, Maha Sarakham, Kalasin, Som Det, Kalasin, Sakon Nakhon, Phong Khon, Udon Thani, Nong Khai, Bueng Gan, Nong Khai, Sang Kham, Pak Chom, Chiang Khan, Loei, Tha Li, Na Haeo, Phitsanulok, Uttaradit, Ban Khok, Na Noi, Nan, Phayao, Chun, Thoeng, Chiang Rai, Phayameng Rai, Phu Chi Fah, Thoeng, Chiang Rai, Phayameng Rai, Chiang Klong, Chiang Rai, Mae Suai, Fang, Chiang Dao, and Chiang Mai.

Due to the pandemic, finding accommodations was challenging. Although I'd been in country for months, locals (not privy to this fact) were afraid of me. Numerous hotels turned me away. At the "end" of a hard day, when the backup accommodation is far away, this becomes problematic. Many resorts/hotels were out of business. At the time, others were closed temporarily.

I intentionally rode 4,500+ miles in order to make this my longest ride. My ride was longer than any two of the 2020 Grand Tours combined. I'm not sure if I'll ever top it. I may by riding from Alaska to Patagonia. I experienced heavy rain on most days. I averaged 80 miles per day.

23. Chiang Mai to Nakhon Phanom Return:
Chiang Mai to Nakhon Phanom, Thailand return

Dates: February 4 to March 5, 2021
My age: 59
Distance: 1,625 miles
Bicycle: Specialized Epic Carbon, mountain bike
Time: 30 days, 19 days of riding
Partner: solo, except Bueng Gan to Nakhon Phanom return with Kig

Notes: I completed this unsupported ride during the COVID-19 pandemic. I rode a route via Chiang Mai, Lamphun, Lampang, Phrae, Den Chai, Uttaradit, Phitsanulok, Nakhon Thai, Loei, Pak Chom, Nong Khai, Si Kai, Bueng Gan, Pak Khat, Bueng Gan, Seka, Nakatae, Nakhon Phanom, Ban Phaeng, Bueng Gan, Nong Khai, San Kom, Loei, Thai Li, Na Haeo, Dan Sai, Nakorn Thai, Chat Trakan, Phitsanulok, Uttaradit, Phrae, Rong Kwang, Ngao, Phayao, Chiang Rai, Mae Suai, Fang, and Chiang Mai.

Over the course of the ride, I put in six days of running, nine centuries, and a biggest day of 134 miles. This was Kig's first multi-day trip. She rode 300+ miles on my old mountain bike. While riding together, we averaged 65 miles per day. On riding days, including those with Kig, I averaged 86 miles.

4. Cycling Races

"I have a hole in my ass. My ass isn't whole."

For my *first* bicycle race, I planned to ride the Race across America (RAAM). This event is billed as "The World's Toughest Bicycle Race." I believe it is. RAAM lurked in the back of my mind for 30 years, having been implanted at Cheryl Marek's fund raiser. When I contacted the RAAM organizers, although eligible based on my palmarès, they suggested I ride a RAAM qualifier. It turned out RAAM wouldn't be my first bicycle race. It ended up being my fourth. I'm one of the least-experienced bicycle racers ever to take on RAAM.

In the first-half century of my life, I never rode a bicycle race. Of course, I never had a cycling coach. The information, which I knew about bicycle racing, was obtained from watching the Tour de France. In the early days, stations never aired entire race stages. My knowledge was limited. When I researched RAAM qualifiers, the Adirondack 540 was the hardest one available. It would be my first race. I ramped up my training. I prepared the best I knew how.

Armed with this background, I list my cycling races.

1. Adirondack 540:
    Wilmington, New York

    Dates: September 13-15, 2012
    My age: 51
    Distance: 544 miles
    Bicycle: Trek Madone 5.5, road bike
    Status: DNF (broken shift lever)
    Time: 32:00:00

Climbing: 20,000 feet completed
Distance completed: 365 miles

Notes: As the name indicates, the race takes place in the Adirondack Mountains in New York State. The Adirondack 540 has 31,000+ feet of climbing in 544 miles. The elevation gain is greater than in climbing Mount Everest from sea level and about three times that of climbing it from base camp. I couldn't assemble a crew in time, so I drove to the race from Maryland alone and competed unsupported. I booked a hotel near the course, so I could visit my room during the four-lap race without losing too much time.

I rode great. The varying terrain and steep climbs required constant shifting. After 365 miles, I broke my rear-derailleur's shift lever. Without a mobile and lacking service anyway, I walked to the first house. The roads were deserted. It was a country mile. I knocked, explained my predicament, and asked to borrow a telephone. The family whom I met were extremely kind. They obliged.

I called the race director John Ceceri. He was busy. Once freed up, John drove to meet me and tried to help. Although he had a full set of tools, John was unable to fix the problem. Without the use of gears, I couldn't ride the climbs. The circumstances dictated that I withdraw. Although terribly disappointed, I felt happy about my performance. If not for the mechanical, I would have finished the race strongly. It was a pleasure befriending John. I vowed to return to finish his demanding race.

2. Florida Cycling Challenge:
   Daytona Beach, Florida

Date: November 11, 2012
My age: 51
Distance: 391 miles
Bicycle: Trek Madone 5.5, road bike
Status: 10:51:00 for 200 miles; 23 hours total riding time
Time: 27:39:00
Distance completed: rode 400+ miles with many wrong turns

Climbing: 5,000 feet

Place: 5th

Notes: Prior to starting RAAM, I wanted a qualifying race under my belt. I signed up for the RAAM Florida Cycling Challenge. I enlisted two Thai friends to support me: Nonglak "Oum" Treethummakul and Pattama "Tui" Longani. The only issues were that they couldn't read maps, spoke limited English, had only one driver's license, couldn't follow directions, and knew nothing about bike racing. We would share an adventure.

I was in great shape. At that time I didn't have a GPS. I intended to follow the leaders and ride with the peloton. For a long time, this strategy worked. I had to ride slower than I wanted. After 100 miles or so, the small pack separated. I explained to Oum and Tui that they needed to drive to the next intersection on the course, wait there, and direct me to go either left or right. Once I passed, they needed to re-pass me, and repeat the process. I suggested holding up a sign with an arrow drawn on it, pointing in the direction that I needed to turn. This would prevent me from needing to slow down too much.

Once I disconnected from other riders, my team made one wrong turn after another. When I went off course, it was time consuming to reunite. I waited at intersections for 15 minutes. Oum and Tui were lost often, but smiling and laughing, whenever and wherever we reconnected. I smiled. I couldn't be competitive. There weren't enough entrants to follow. There was no peloton. I simply needed to finish.

Once competing wasn't possible, I took responsibility for map reading. While taking as much time as necessary, I stopped and figured out our route. Due to the crazy number of turns, I stopped frequently. Oum and Tui became tired. At night we struggled to see road signs, locking our eyes in a squint. When I finally finished, we joked about the wrong turns. Thanks to Oum and Tui, I qualified for RAAM.

3.   Doi Inthanon Climb:

Chiang Mai, Thailand

Date: February 3, 2013
My age: 51
Distance: 48.5K (30.1 miles)
Bicycle: Trek Madone 5.5, road bike
Time: 3:08:00
Climbing: 7,720 feet
Place: 53rd
Riders: 700

Notes: The 8,415-foot high Doi Inthanon, which is the highest mountain in Thailand, is considered one of the hardest climbs in Asia. By some sources, it ranks in the top-100 hardest climbs in the world. The climb via Route 1009 gains almost one and a half vertical miles. Near the finish, the road pitches to 23%. There are long sections with gradients over 17%. Each year in February, riders take on Doi Inthanon. Many end up walking. It's the only bicycle race I rode which wasn't an individual time trial. This race allowed drafting.

As an avid cycling fan, whenever I got a chance, I watched the Tour de France. Announcers Phil Ligget and the late Paul Sherwen said: "If you want to win a bike race, you've got to stay near the front." I rode at the front. At the first point where the road went sharply uphill, three riders broke away. I heard Phil and Paul's voices reprimanding riders who let a break go up the road.

In a Herculean effort, while using the last of my glycogen reserves, I closed the gap to the breakaway. As soon as I reached the third rider's back wheel, a group of 30+ riders flew past. I towed them to the breakaway. Already on the limit after only 10 miles, I suffered for the next 20 miles. My lower-back pain was intense. I finished 53rd.

Although I believed I could climb with the best, and this race attracts professionals, I was wrong, perhaps more wrong than I've ever been in my life! I shouldn't have listened to Phil and Paul, but instead listened to my body and ridden my own pace. I could have finished 30 minutes sooner and been in the top 20. I wouldn't have suffered to the extent that I did. This race taught me valuable lessons.

Due to the steepness of the road, few riders descend the mountain on their bicycles. I did. It's dangerous.

4. Race Across America (RAAM):
   Oceanside, California to Annapolis, Maryland

Dates: June 12-23, 2013
My age: 51
Distance: 2,962 miles
Bicycles: Trek Madone 5.5 and Specialized S-Works Roubaix, road bikes
Time: 12 days, 1 hour, and 57 minutes
Climbing: 160,000+ feet
Place: 23rd (unofficial)
Riders: 45

Notes: I arrived at RAAM in the best shape of my life. My training in the heat, humidity, and mountains of Thailand had gone incredibly well. I put in some fantastic rides, including a few mentioned in the chapter on cycling rides. My team consisted of a group of five great friends. We noticed other crews were much larger. They noticed my crew was the smallest. Other teams questioned the sanity of having such a small crew. I felt lucky to have five friends with me. We only had four drivers for our SUV and RV. Our problems began immediately.

At the staggered start, riders are released at one-minute intervals. On the initial, controlled section of the course, which is ten miles long, my mandatory rear light popped off. After hitting the ground, it shattered into pieces. The batteries went flying. Throughout this section of the course, I obeyed the 15-mph speed limit, but the rider behind caught me. While I searched for the batteries and reassembled the light, he became angry. No overtaking is permitted in the parade section.

On the first day, I suffered terrible diarrhea. When racing 3,000 miles in extreme conditions, diarrhea on day one spells trouble. Then in Arizona, my SUV's battery died—drained by faulty wiring in the speaker system a friend had rigged so that I could listen to music while riding. At night a rider can't proceed without direct follow, so I needed to stop riding, until that problem was resolved. It took a while to install a spare. Luckily, I'd planned for this contingency.

We faced problems with navigation. My efforts to use a GPS failed. It had me taking shortcuts and missing turns. The granularity of the shortest-path algorithm in my GPS unit was out of kilter with the one used to describe the route. The race tries to avoid main roads. The route book was 55 pages long. Each page contained about 20 lines of directions. When exhausted, it became more difficult to follow the course.

Drivers and crew members had trouble completing simple tasks. Driver: "Did you say left or right?" Crew member giving directions: "I don't remember." After rechecking: "Go left." Driver: "Which way?" Crew member: "Didn't I say right?" Driver: "I'm not sure." Crew Member: "Let me check." Driver: "Okay, let me know." Such discussions were repeated over and over. Memory failed. Vision blurred. We felt exhausted after just two days. All teams are confronted with similar issues. Larger teams get more sleep. Rookies don't fare too well.

Riders encounter extreme heat in the desert with temperatures in the shade exceeding 120°F. There's no shade on the course. When my crew lagged behind and I reached a fork in the road, I waited for them to provide directions. I shook my head. I craned and squinted. I wondered what went wrong. While waiting, dehydration from my diarrhea worsened. Once my crew arrived, they filled my empty water bottles. I ate Swedish fish. I listened to their troubles. I continued.

I developed hot spots on my feet. The absurdly high temperatures in the desert caused swelling. A crumbling section of road in California being readied for repaving was responsible for the start of my bloody saddle sores. They bled all the way to Annapolis. The roof of my mouth sunburned. Due to low humidity, I suffered bloody noses. My knees ached. Whenever we stopped, I iced. One time, everyone fell asleep while I was icing. I woke up with frozen knees. I worried.

I could handle any three environmental issues at a time, for example, a head wind, a rough road surface, and rain. When four or more things went wrong simultaneously, I struggled. Although the deck seemed stacked against me, I knew it wasn't really. I knew things had to improve. The count would drop back down to three soon enough. I never thought of quitting. It wasn't an option.

I experienced an unusual number of flats. At one point while changing tires, my crew accidentally left my $3,000 Zipp wheels behind. I kept suggesting we switch to these more aerodynamic wheels. My crew remained silent. I gave up after a couple days of trying to persuade them. I figured they had their reasons. Amazingly, a few days later, another RAAM crew found and returned my wheels. We made use of the Zipp wheels. The crew felt relieved. We grinned at each other.

When my entire bike started to shimmy, I almost crashed on a high-speed descent in Utah. I yelled many expletives. I learned my crew members had thought I was going to die, too. They had been screaming. I don't know if the shimmy was caused by a loose headset or an improperly tightened hub. After that incident and worsening numbness in my hands, I feared descending at super-high speeds, especially while riding down switchbacks in darkness.

A couple times crew members almost quit. I stopped to rally them, providing words of encouragement. I ate dinner with them. My crew did a remarkable job. Sleep deprivation pushed us to our limits. Several storms battered us, where I wasn't able to ride due to nearby lightning strikes, gale-force winds, and flooding.

Throughout the race, my crew remained in close contact with race headquarters. My team told me that I was going to finish on time. When I crossed the line in Annapolis, they exclaimed: "You finished RAAM, Ray!" Those words were music to my ears. My crew was so proud of me, and vice versa. Team Greenlaw finished RAAM. We were in the house in the nick of time.

Although exhausted beyond human limits, we felt satisfied. We did it. We made it. We achieved our goal. While sleeping very little for 12 days, the smallest crew had surmounted all obstacles. Relieved, everyone hugged and backslapped. We were giddy. We needed to nap. Shortly thereafter, the race director approached me. I awaited his congratulations. I smiled. He told me I hadn't finished. I didn't ask why. My crew had convinced me that I was an official finisher. We were all heartbroken.

I gave everything to the race. Although I wanted to be an official finisher, I had to be satisfied with my maximum-effort performance. I felt bad for my crew; they felt bad for me. No one who races RAAM wants to be given anything, ever. It's a cruel event. The racers are the strongest, toughest, and most dedicated people whom I've met. The race is legendary, as are its stories of human endurance, commitment, and suffering. Although no one thought that I would return, I knew that I would. I wanted to become an official RAAM finisher, completing the course just barely over the time limit left me with an uneasy feeling.

More details about the race can be found in my RAAM 2013 blog, which is linked from my website.

5. Adirondack 540:
Wilmington, New York

Dates: September 13-15, 2013
My age: 52
Distance: 544 miles
Bicycle: Specialized S-Works Roubaix, road bike
Time: 41:27:00
Distance completed: 544 miles
Climbing: 31,000+ feet
Place: 1st

Notes: When I returned to the Adirondack 540 after my broken shift-lever DNF ride, I was in outstanding shape. After RAAM, I felt confident. Fish, my crew chief from RAAM, and Oum made up my team. Oum had been with me at the Florida 400. While crewing for me at RAAM, she did a phenomenal job. I could never ask for a more dedicated and outstanding crew member than Oum. She gave her all.

Although it was cold, rainy, and windy, I rode a fast race. After 140 miles of riding, I injured my left eye. For the remainder of the race, I relied on my right eye. With monocular vision, depth perception becomes a serious problem. Descending mountain passes in the dark became scary. On one descent, a black bear crossed the road in front of me. I avoided hitting him or crashing.

My crew stayed up all night and did a great job. Thanks, Oum and Fish. I handily won in difficult conditions. It was a nice feeling. John Ceceri was there to greet me, and we caught up. My team was so exhausted that we couldn't party. The next day we completed the drive back to Maryland. I returned to work. Students said I looked tired. I was.

6. Race Across America (RAAM):
Oceanside, California to Annapolis, Maryland

Dates: June 11-22, 2014
My age: 52
Distance: 3,020 miles
Bicycles: Specialized S-Works Roubaix, road bike; Specialized Shiv, time-trial bike
Time: 11 days, 22 hours, and 45 minutes
Climbing: 160,000+ feet
Place: 23rd
Riders: 48

Notes: After my experience at RAAM in 2013, no one thought I would return a year later. Costing me $50,000 to participate, the expense was a financial burden. I didn't want to trouble my crew again, as they already had made great sacrifices. They pushed beyond their limits in 2013. I never wanted them to dig that deep again. I didn't want to see my friends sleep deprived.

My bike mechanic and friend Brad "Wrench" Phillips, my crew chief Fish, my dear friend Oum, and Huck Lem returned for a second attempt with me at RAAM. They wouldn't have missed this opportunity for anything. They went all in and wanted me to become an official finisher. Although my mentor Aceman wasn't able to join us, he was there in spirit. He followed along, helping out from the sidelines.

This time I brought a larger crew that included two Naval Academy Midshipmen: Zachary "Zac" Dannelly and William "Bill" Young. Also along were Wilson "Google" McAllister, Shigeki "Shagg" Makino, Al "The Photographer" Peasley, Andrew "Slacker" Slack, and Erick "The Kid" Banke from Annapolis Cycle. My friends Tarman and Helen "Ironwoman" Göransson, who were with me for part of my first attempt, were there in spirit, as was my friend Marjorie Roxburgh, who supported us after both races.

My training in Thailand went great, until I was hit by a motorcycle in late January. I broke my collarbone. In the Tour de France, I watched riders carry on with broken collarbones. I got back on my bike and started riding. No! It wasn't possible. The pain was too great. I worried about doing more damage. I rode three days later though, and within six weeks, I was healed The doctor said I healed like a 12-year old. Professional cyclists are tough athletes, and (professional) cycling is one of the world's most dangerous sports.

This time Fish would be there for the entire race. He wanted me to help me to an official finish. My team had more experience, and we had far more help. The course was 60 miles longer though, and due to my shoulder injury, I wasn't as fit. However, with two thirds of RAAM complete, I was ten hours ahead of the cutoff time. We weren't breathing easily though. When stormy weather hit, my cushion disappeared. I pedaled. To the extent possible, I ignored Mother Nature.

On the final day in Maryland, I had no time to spare. When I got two flat tires, my dream faded. Two riders passed me. I was terribly exhausted. I needed a rest, as did my crew. At the last timing cutoff, I told the crew that I needed to sleep a couple hours. I was weaving all over the road. After what seemed like only 15 minutes, they woke me up and assured me I'd been down for two hours. I carried on like a zombie. I made it to the finish with just over an hour to spare. I thought that I was official, and I was. The race director warmly congratulated me. He smiled. He understood what finishing RAAM meant to me, especially after the previous year's heartbreak.

I owe a great debt of gratitude to my crew, especially those team members who came back a second time and believed in me. Their experience and understanding of the race were incredibly helpful to me and to other new crew members. I'm forever thankful to this team for their giving, kindness, and unbreakable spirits, especially Oum. She did a remarkable job. Oum showed me the meaning of service, teamwork, kindness, and unselfishness. She showed me what life and love are all about. I'll never forget.

A few years later I was told that I'd slept for only 15 minutes at the last RAAM checkpoint. When I learned this fact, I shook my head. If the team had allowed me the sleep that I craved, I would have missed the cutoff. Their white lie kept me in the game. It was an incredible team effort. I thanked my crew member for revealing this secret. We laughed.

When I meet people in bicycle shops and cyclists from around the world, they tell me excitedly: "I never thought I'd meet a RAAM finisher." I'm one of about 40 men over age 50 to complete RAAM in under 12 days. I have scars on my ass, numbness in my hands, and nerve damage in my feet to remind me. The experience and what I gained from RAAM is far more important than what I lost. I don't ever plan on doing anything as hard as RAAM again. It was almost a bridge too far. I suppose that's the point.

More details about the race can be found in my RAAM 2014 blog, which is linked from my website.

7. Adirondack 540:
   Wilmington, New York

Dates: September 12-14, 2014
My age: 53
Distance: 544 miles
Bicycle: Specialized S-Works Roubaix, road bike
Time: 17:00:00
Distance completed: 272 miles
Climbing: 16,500+ feet
Place: DNF

Notes: John Ceceri made this edition of the Adirondack 540 the race of champions. All former winners were invited back and given free entry. After my win the previous year and my finish at RAAM, I was considered a favorite. I was in great shape, as I somehow found the motivation to continue training.

Race day brought cold, rain, and fierce winds. I led the race comfortably at 225 miles. My legs felt good. However, I lost vision in my left eye, and I needed to squint to see out of my right eye. I took a break and put in eye drops, but my vision didn't improve. I feel disappointed to drop out of any race, but it hurt even more to drop out of one that I was winning. I couldn't see. There was no choice. I didn't finish. Over the next week, my vision gradually returned to normal.

If I ride another endurance race, I'll wear goggles rather than eyeglasses. I believe that my corneas dried out. I don't know if this condition is related to my Lasik surgery from years earlier. Few eye doctors are familiar with the problem. My research showed me that another ultra-cyclist suffered from a similar issue. I'm sure that dehydration, as well as the weather, plays a big role. When your eyes fail, you're definitely on the limit.

8. <u>World Time Trial Championships:</u>
   Borrego Springs, California

Date: November 5, 2016
My age: 55
Distance: 117.6 miles

Bicycle: Specialized Shiv, time-trial bike
Time: 6 hours
Age group: 2nd
Overall men: 6th

Notes: My race started at noon. It was hot in the Anza-Borrego Desert. I raced the six-hour event. In this race you ride as far as you can in six hours. Kig supported me. I bought an aero water-bottle cage for this race. On the rough roads within five miles, my water bottle popped out of its pricey new cage. In the desert heat, I needed to stop and retrieve it. Designed to save me 30 seconds, the cage ended up costing me a couple minutes.

The course consisted of two distinct loops—a hilly loop of 19 miles and a short loop of 4.8 miles. I rode well. Only full loops, which are completed within six hours, are counted. After four and a half hours, riders move from the big to the small loop. Because I couldn't utilize my aero cage, I became progressively more dehydrated. Each time I rode past, Kig handed me drinks and snacks. One time I came to a complete stop and emptied two entire bottles. The amount of salt on my shirt concerned me. A group of fans in the pit area braved the heat to cheer on competitors.

As I returned for the penultimate time, someone yelled there was sufficient time to complete another short loop. Due to heat exhaustion and my concentration on riding, I wasn't keeping track of timing as well as I should have been. I pushed hard to make sure my last loop counted. Nearing the finish, the 24-hour world-record holder, five-time RAAM champion, and RAAM course-record holder Christoph Strasser passed me. He was finishing the 24-hour race and had started 18 hours earlier than me!

I couldn't believe how fast Christoph flew by me. Mesmerized by his speed, I didn't think about the fact that he was trying to beat the clock on his last lap. The great man averaged 23.5 mph for the entire 24-hour race. I pressed on harder, inspired by this magnificent athlete. On the last loop, I finished a few seconds behind Christoph and exactly two seconds over the time limit. None of my last 4.8 miles counted. Christoph had motored in and his last lap counted.

Fortunately, being unable to count the last 4.8 miles didn't impact my placing. It sure would have been nice to count it though. In fact, when I finished, I heard my final lap did count. Later, I was informed it didn't … I thought back to my "time-saving" water-bottle cage. Although my final lap wasn't counted, the memory of Christoph flying be me is one that I won't forget. I won't forget the times that he passed me at RAAM either. RAAM riders start at one-minute intervals in decreasing order of their numbers, which are assigned for life. Christoph raced RAAM many years before me. To race against the GOAT (Greatest of All Time) is a special experience.

5. Mountaineering

"Are you kidding me?"

When I was 14, in an effort to meet girls, Fish and I joined a religious youth group on their trip to climb Mount Monadnock in New Hampshire. I didn't fall in love with a girl, but I did fall in love with mountains. After that experience I began climbing in the White Mountains of New Hampshire. I feel at home and at peace in mountains. When I possessed the financial resources to travel freely, I started climbing bigger mountains. I traveled the world to climb high peaks. I climbed in the Swiss and Italian Alps, often with Tarman. I became a good climber, honing my skills on steep, snowy slopes and icy glaciers. Tarman and I took on the seven summits.

I started wearing glasses as a teenager. In the mountains, my glasses fogged up. It became difficult to see. Sometimes ice formed on my lenses. I carried defogger. When I removed my glasses, I had trouble seeing. In snowy conditions my vision was hampered severely. If I broke or lost my glasses, I would be in trouble. My left eye was only 20/800. When the opportunity presented itself, I opted for Lasik surgery. Within days of surgery, my left eye was 20/25 and my right eye 20/20 from 20/250. Having near perfect vision made climbing mountains even more enjoyable. After my successful surgery, Tarman had Lasik.

I climbed about 1,500 mountains across seven continents. Examples are Pico de Orizaba in Mexico, the Matterhorn on the border of Switzerland and Italy, Mount Olympus in Greece, and Mount Rainier in Washington State. I climbed the highest mountain in many countries and US states. In my palmarès, I list only those mountains that are part of the seven summits. These are the best-known peaks I climbed.

1. Mount Elbrus:
   Russia, Europe

   Summit date: July 24, 2001
   My age: 39
   Elevation: 18,481 feet
   Partner: Paul Göransson

   Notes: I summited Mount Elbrus with Tarman. This was the first of my seven summits. Until I was close to the summit, I never felt any effects from the altitude. We broke trail in deep snow. We ascended 6,500 feet on summit day, leaving from the "barrels." We enjoyed a wonderful trip to Russia, and when we weren't climbing, we spent time sightseeing and drinking vodka. I lied. They offered us vodka while climbing, too. A highlight for both of us was our tour of the Kremlin. Our Russian guide didn't speak English, but he spoke Spanish, so we communicated in Spanish.

2. Aconcagua:
   Argentina, South America

   Summit date: January 9, 2002
   My age: 40
   Elevation: 22,840 feet
   Partner: Paul Göransson, André Imboden, and other Swiss alpinists

   Notes: We spent too little time acclimatizing, and as a result, some group members failed to summit. Due to pulmonary edema, Tarman was evacuated by mule from our 14,000-foot basecamp. Seeing my best friend ride off on a mule in a storm, while he struggled to breathe, caused gut-wrenching pain. I worried about him. While his mule stared straight ahead, he looked back. I waved good-bye. He safely arrived in Maine after an arduous, solo journey, including a hospital stay in Chile.

André and I ascended 5,320 feet from Nido de Condores on summit day. It was a long push. We both got frostbite on our faces, as Viento Blanco (the White Wind) and the Caneleta challenged us. Once back at base camp, we met a hardened team of Mexican climbers. They failed to reach the summit. We also met a group of Austrians. They came to Aconcagua after going to 8,750 meters on Mount Everest. They too failed on Aconcagua. When I saw the experienced groups failing on the mountain at the same as I succeeded, I felt lucky.

After the trip I toured Argentina. Due to political instability, the Argentinian peso collapsed. There were street riots. The aftermath turned out to be as dangerous as the climb. I felt happy to be heading home, but I planned to return to learn more about the culture, enjoy the wonderful food and wine, and of course, visit Iguazu Falls. Since that 2002 trip, I traveled to Argentina a handful of times, most recently in 2019, and done exactly what I dreamed. I crave their bife de chorizo, gelato, and ceviche. I miss the wonderful people.

3. Mount Kilimanjaro:
    Tanzania, Africa

Summit date: August 3, 2002
My age: 41
Elevation: 19,339 feet
Partner: Eugene

Notes: Due to flight delays and lost luggage in Nairobi, Kenya, I arrived later than intended in Moshi. Eugene and I accelerated our schedule. We summited Mount Kilimanjaro in just four days. I traveled alone from Savannah, Georgia, which has an elevation of ten feet above sea level. We climbed the "whiskey" route. On the summit while I suffered from a headache and altitude sickness, Eugene smoked a cigarette. I moved up wind. We laughed.

On the day we summited, after a vertical mile, we descended two vertical miles. As part of my trip, I went to Ngorongoro Crater,

Olduvai Gorge, Lake Manyara National Park, and other interesting places. Fond memories of Tanzania fill my mind.

4. Mount Kosciusko:
   New South Wales, Australia

   Summit date: March 17, 2003
   My age: 41
   Elevation: 7,310 feet
   Partners: Göransson family

   Notes: On our flight out of LA, due to a problem with our airplane's wing, we arrived a day late for our climb. Because of the additional ten hours of flying, we were exhausted. On the long trip from Sydney to the south, I drove through kangaroo territory. The weather was good, and the climb was easy. Once back in Sydney, I climbed the Sydney Harbor Bridge with the teenagers Jennie and Peter Göransson. We went to Cairns, from where Tarman and I dove the Great Barrier Reef. It was a great trip; one we think about often.

5. Vinson Massif:
   Sentinel Range of the Ellsworth Mountains, Antarctica

   Summit date: January 10, 2005
   My age: 43
   Elevation: 16,067 feet
   Partners: John Rust, and Paul and Peter Göransson

   Notes: Prior to the trip, I spent a couple weeks hiking in Patagonia with Scott Woolums. He was our expedition leader. We traveled to Antarctica with Scott. The flights to and from Antarctic were amazing. The climb was frigid. John was incredibly strong. He and I bookended our rope team with Peter and Paul in the middle. We moved well as a unit. It was a proud moment to summit with my friends. We descended safely in frigid temperatures.

As a result of frostbite, one mountaineer whom we met lost an eye and another lost his nose. I'll never forget the nice guy with a hole in the front of his face asking: "Does anyone know the score in the Patriots game?" I shook my head. I couldn't help but wonder if he'd looked in a mirror. He's a positive individual. No one knew the score in the game. Few cared.

After our epic summit push on Vinson, we became stranded at Patriot Hills. We climbed nearby peaks but worried about our dwindling food supplies. When a small window of calm presented itself, our brave Russian pilots came in and flew us back to Ushuaia. The takeoff and flight were scary. After what we'd been through, the non-glacial landing in Tierra del Fuego felt safe. We were relieved to step on solid, non-icy ground again.

I went sightseeing and drank pisco sours in Punta Arenas. After unwinding, I completed the remaining six flights required to get home. The airline needed to attach two baggage-claim strips, as one can't accommodate that number of connecting flights. When we climbed Vinson, only around 400 people had ever been there. The logistics of such trips were still being ironed out.

6. Mount McKinley:
   Alaska, North America

Summit date: May 26, 2009
My age: 47
Elevation: 20,320 feet
Partners: Rainer Mountain Guides group

Notes: This climb was my sixth of the seven summits. When I climbed, several people died on the mountain. A blizzard dumped four feet of snow. Winds gusting to hurricane force created huge drifts. In treacherous avalanche conditions, we roped up with two other teams. Our group of 12 climbers took 11 hours to descend one mile of the route.

Many mountaineers suffered frostbite. I yelled at one climber who lost his will to continue. He made it back. He thanked me. At the airplane hangar, our team celebrated with groups of international climbers. We felt glad to be safe. Following our descent, I learned the mountain closed for several weeks. During that period, no one else summited.

I've thought about climbing Mount Everest. And, on a trip to Nepal, I saw the mountain. I flew past it a few times. Over the years I contacted guiding companies and organized my gear for the climb. But, I never made the commitment. One detraction is the crowds. The other is the cost. Perhaps these are excuses. Major closures of the mountain, after big avalanches and the COVID-19 pandemic, have postponed any plans that I was formulating.

If I ever make the commitment, the mountain will be there. I would love to complete the seven summits and stand on the highest point on Earth. Like all climbers, I need to weigh the costs and risks against the benefits. So far, the balance hasn't tipped in the right direction. I'm in touch with Sherpa friends, so time will tell. My clock is running out. No decision is a decision.

6. Ultra-Marathons

"I lost eight toenails."

Dave Wottle inspired my brother to take up competitive running, and the two of them inspired me. When I was 11 years old, I started run training. Over the past 50 years, I ran 100,000+ miles. There was a time when I ran morning, noon, and night. I got called Forrest Gump. I took one day off per week. My biggest weeks exceeded 125 miles. I increased the length of long runs. My longest training run is 75 miles. I stretched and did yoga to combat tightening muscles.

My childhood friend Claire became a world-class marathoner. We reconnected on the opposite coast, while both attending graduate school at the University of Washington. As I mentioned in the introduction, Claire's friend Kim Moody was an outstanding ultra-marathoner. Kim ran a 6:01 for 50 miles in 1986. Her time still ranks high on the all-time list. During our long runs, I learned from Claire that any race over 50K (31.1 miles) is called an *ultra-marathon*. Her stories about Kim inspired me to run ultras.

Before delving into my list of ultras, a few quick facts are in order. I set my best time for 50 miles of 6:27:05 at the Texas Trail 50, which is run on trails. Although not nearly as fast as Kim, a 7:45 pace per mile on trails is a solid effort. At the Western States 100, I set my best for 100 miles in 22:13:20. When training days are included, I went the ultra-distance or farther 254 times. Those runs alone exceeded 10,000 miles. I had countless efforts between 26.2 and 31 miles, but I follow Claire's definition of ultra.

I won my age group at the competitive Texas Trail 50. I finished in the top-ten overall at the following races: Laugavegurinn 55K, the Mountain Masochist 50 (two times), the Nifty Fifty, the Nugget 50, the

Strolling Jim (two times), the Texas Trail 50 (four times), and the US Nationals 100K Championships.

I completed six 100-mile runs and thirteen 50-mile runs. The hardest race I ever completed was the Wasatch Front 100, which has 47,300 feet of elevation change, or almost exactly nine vertical miles of up and down. I lost eight toenails in that race. All the 100-mile runs I completed were at high altitude. Living at sea-level made these special accomplishments.

While in graduate school, Claire told me about the Western States 100. In order to gain entry into that race, the Grand Daddy of all ultra-marathons, I needed to qualify by running a 50-mile race. I chose the Sunmart Texas Trail 50 for my first ultra. I finished third. That thrust me into a period where I would run ultra-marathons during three decades. Although I don't race ultras anymore, I do sometimes go out for 35-mile training runs. When I'm hiking, I often exceed the ultra-distance. I enjoy covering a long distance on foot. Maybe there's something etched in my DNA from the great human migrations.

Next I present a few facts about my personal records (PRs) and a summary of my wins and top-ten placings.

Personal records:
- PR 50 miles: 6:27:05 at the Texas Trail 50, 1997
- PR 100K: 8:20:43 at the US Nationals 100K, 1998
- PR 100 miles: 22:13:20 at the Western States 100, 1994

Wins:
- Age group at Texas Trail 50

Top ten:
- Laugavegurinn 55K
- Mountain Masochist (2 times)
- Nifty Fifty
- Nugget 50
- Strolling Jim (2 times)
- Texas Trail 50 (4 times)

- US Nationals 100K Championships

Basic stats:
- Number of 100-mile runs completed: 6
- Number of 50-mile runs completed: 13
- Number of times going the ultra-distance (50K or farther): 254
- Hardest race: Wasatch Front 100

In what follows I list my ultra-marathons.

1. Sunmart Texas Trail 50:
   Huntsville, Texas

   Date: December 15, 1990
   My age: 29
   Distance: 50.2 miles
   Time: 7:17:15
   Place: 3rd
   Finishers: 57

   Notes: In my first 50-mile run, I started out conservatively, not knowing what to expect. I passed runners throughout. I came close to second place. I finished strongly in third. Strangely, this would be my only podium finish in an ultra-marathon.[1] Of course, at the time I figured that in the near future I would win an ultra. The deep fatigue caused by such a long run put me in a peaceful state. Post-race I enjoyed an excellent BBQ and celebration, and for the time being, I was hooked on ultra-marathoning.

2. Western States 100 Mile Endurance Run:
   Squaw Valley, California

   Date: June 29, 1991
   My age: 29

---

[1] See notes on the Nugget 50.

Distance: 100 miles
Time: 26:33:02
Place: 130th
Finishers: 242

Notes: With a single ultra-marathon under my belt, I decided to take on one of the hardest runs in the world—the Western States 100 and its 41,060 feet of elevation change. I once did a training run of 75 miles with my friend Randy "Gumby" Day, but that was the only time I'd gone farther than 50 miles. I hadn't done eight vertical miles in a day. The temperature fluctuates 100°F on race day, which if you think about it, is absurd. I couldn't afford to think about it. I didn't dwell on the difficulty of the race. I trained hard. I wanted to finish.

I drove to the race from New Hampshire on my own. I reasoned that if I could run for 24 hours straight then I could drive for 24 hours straight. I hadn't proven yet that I could run for 24 hours straight. My logic was flawed. I only spent 54 hours getting to the race. Google lists the drive as taking 44 hours and covering 2,965 miles. The company didn't exist until six years after my race. I had no clue how long the drive would take. When I exited my truck, my knees hurt. I shook my head. With a sore back and stiff legs, I would take on my hardest athletic challenge to date. I hobbled to the pre-race meeting. I should have flown to California.

After the 5:00 AM start up the ski slopes at Squaw Valley, at sunrise I turned around for a magnificent view of Lake Tahoe. Due to the frigid temperatures, I only admired the view for a moment. I was in a race. I gulped the thin air. I ran behind Anne Trason, who's the greatest female ultra-marathoner of all-time. She set 20 world records and won the Western States 100 a record 14 times. I was out of my league. I had no idea Anne would become the greatest of all-time. She was the overall winner at many races. Anne disappeared on a long downhill. During the race, I never saw her again. She won the women's race and finished ninth overall behind a strong men's field.

I wasn't used to running all night. Inspired by the ultra-marathoning greats, such as Anne, Tom Johnson, Ted Corbitt, and Chuck Jones, I dug deep. The altitude, heat, river crossings, scree, fast pace, and other factors made for a memorable experience, as had the moment of silence at the start of the race for the runner who'd been killed on the course a few weeks earlier by a mountain lion. While running alone at night, I felt scared. I listened for growls.

After my successful finish, I took a week to drive back across the US via a southern route. In the last 24 hours in a push to get home, I covered 1,750 miles. I felt sore from the race. When I exited my truck, I hunched. While unpacking, I shuffled with straight legs. In the weeks following the race, I lost five toenails. My feet were by no means the worst that I'd seen. The other runners whom I met were tremendous inspirations. I planned to resume training as soon as possible. I planned to train harder.

The finishing percentages aren't high for 100-mile runs, especially for rookies. The weather is a determining factor. In extreme heat, more runners drop out. One third to half the field doesn't finish. A good crew can help tremendously, but I ran crewless. I carried my truck key the entire distance. I made a poster of me fording the American River, which my Mom displayed. Claire was proud of me. My Dad got a finisher's T-shirt. I told stories about the race and the epic drive. I finished one of the hardest 100-miles in the world. I ran 100 miles!

3. Sunmart Texas Trail 50:
    Huntsville, Texas

    Date: December 7, 1991
    My age: 30
    Distance: 50.2 miles
    Time: 7:48:49
    Place: 10th
    Finishers: 73

Notes: With two ultras under my belt, I planned to enter the Texas Trail 50 again and go for the win. As a result of my early fast pace, going through the marathon in three hours, I faltered in the latter half. Although 30 minutes slower than my first ultra, I learned valuable lessons. I learned that if you want to win, you have to risk losing or even dropping out. I learned that running 25 miles with an empty tank isn't much fun. I learned that the longer a race is the more important the pace is.

4. Leadville Trail 100:
   Leadville, Colorado

Date: August 15, 1992
My age: 31
Distance: 100 miles
Time: DNF, dropped out at Twin Lakes, 61 miles in 15:19:10
Finishers: 138
50 mile split: 9:40:57

Notes: The Leadville Trail 100 has 31,200 feet of elevation change, a minimum altitude of 9,200 feet, and a max of 12,600. I went out hard and was in the top ten at 50 miles. My split time was 9:40:57. I covered half the course in 30% of the allotted time. The altitude bothered me. I sat down and tried to recover. I failed. I progressed slowly. I stopped. I continued. I put my hands on my knees. I vomited. I took five and a half hours to cover the next 11 miles.

In half the allotted time, I completed 60% of the race. I needed to go 39 miles in 15 hours. I was over the hardest climb. Night approached. Temperatures dropped. I had no pacer. I continued vomiting from altitude sickness. I smelled horrendous. I evaluated my predicament. The prognosis wasn't good. I felt weak and broken. I dropped out at Twin Lakes at mile 61 in a time of 15:19:10.

Later I felt angry for giving up. I never had quit anything. If I had a crew, I thought I would have finished. I became better at asking others for help. I realized these difficult endurance events required support crews. I couldn't do it alone. I needed to train at altitude. I vowed to return and have a better performance.

5. Mountain Masochist Trail Run:
   Blue Ridge Parkway, Virginia

   Date: October 24, 1992
   My age: 31
   Distance: 50 miles
   Time: 7:58:00 (approximate)
   Place: 7th
   Finishers: 155 (approximate)

   Notes: This race has 16,200 feet of elevation change. I ran a solid race and finished in the top ten. My friend David "The Runner" Horton was the race director. We competed together often. It was nice to catch up. Later David broke my FKT for the PCT. Before he made his record attempt, I provided him with guidance and suggestions.

6. Sunmart Texas Trail 50:
   Huntsville, Texas

   Date: December 19, 1992
   My age: 31
   Distance: 50.2 miles
   Time: 6:47:25
   Place: 10th
   Finishers: 139

   Notes: It was fun to run at this event, as I'd become friends with the organizers and regulars. I ran an excellent race on the trails and averaged 8:07 pace per mile.

7. Nugget 50:
   North San Juan, California

Date: May 22, 1993
My age: 31
Distance: 50 miles
Time: 4:52:00
Place: 1st in the 36 miler (tie)
Finishers: 72

Notes: This race had a crazy ending. I planned to race the Nugget 50 to win, as first place received automatic entry (normally by lottery only) into the Western States 100. There was deep snow on the course. I was stopped by race officials at mile 18 for 13 minutes. Officials weren't sure what to do: allow runners to proceed or direct them to turn around. Although the original plan called for an aid station ahead, it wouldn't be there. No vehicles could pass. Runners would be on their own. Safety became a concern.

Eventually, five runners gathered. The early arrivals got cold. The organizers finally made the official decision to change the race to a 36-mile, out-and-back run. We accepted that decision. I pressed on hard with Brian Purcell—a former winner of the Western States 100, the Westfield (a 544-mile ultra in Australia), and many other ultras. We chatted. Brian was one of the top ultra-runners in the world, tough as nails. I hung on for grim death.

When we reached 31 miles, Brian and I were stopped again. This time a different official told us the race had changed to a 50 miler over a different route. With the wishy-washy officiating, Brian and I decided to run the 36 miler, as did many others. We finished tied for first, shaking our heads in disbelief about what had transpired. Although we didn't gain an entry into the Western States 100, I enjoyed running with and getting to know Brian. Accounting for stoppage time, we averaged 7:40 pace per mile over the mountainous route.

8. Leadville Trail 100:
    Leadville, Colorado

Date: August 21, 1993
My age: 32
Distance: 100 miles
Time: 23:53:48
Place: 24th
Finishers: 134

Notes: I returned to Leadville in an attempt to avenge my earlier DNF. I ran a great race and was in the top ten with 12 miles to go. Tarman paced me. I ran in racing flats, as trail-running shoes hadn't been invented yet. My feet were incredibly sore. We ended up walking much of the last part. I lost 15 places in the process. For a flatlander I dealt well with the high elevation and ranked near the top of those who didn't live at altitude.

The awards given at 100-mile trail runs are belt buckles. I won the coveted, WWF-sized, sterling-silver, Leadville Trail 100 buckle for finishing in under 25 hours. I keep it with my other 100-mile trail awards. I don't wear the buckle for two reasons: 1) it's so big that when you bend over you injure an organ, and 2) the silver needs frequent polishing. It's a nice award and a reminder of a tough day—one in which I succeeded, where I failed previously. The award binds Tarman and me together in yet another adventure.

I returned to the Leadville Trail 100 two more times. I paced Tarman in a failed attempt. Then I paced him again to a successful finish. I was incredibly happy to be part of his crew. I was proud of him. He dug deep to make the cutoff.

9. Angeles Crest 100 Mile Endurance Run:
   Wrightwood, California

Date: October 9, 1993
My age: 32
Distance: 100 miles
Time: DNF, dropped out at Chantry Flats, 76 miles in 17:11:00
Finishers: 58

Notes: I made an attempt to win this race and started out fast with the leader, Fred Shufflebarger. He lives in Southern California and trained on the course regularly. Fred knew the trails. It was a big mistake, but while it was dark, I had to stay with Fred or I would have been totally lost. When I went to the bathroom, Fred dropped me. I made wrong turns that cost me time. I vomited. I became dehydrated. I lost toenails. I sat down for an hour. Almost no one passed me. I debated what to do.

When I reached Chantry Flats at mile 76, I was still in the top ten. The cutoff time for the race is 33 hours. I had 16 hours to go 24 miles. However, facing nighttime without support, suffering from bad feet, and feeling weak from hours of vomiting, I decided to quit. I dropped out after 17 hours. Due to redlining my effort in an attempt to win, I went too deep. I cracked. My will broke. I could have slept for eight hours and walked to the finish.

Fred ended up winning. I pushed him for 30 miles. His time stands as one of the fastest ever. I vowed to return. I planned to run more sensibly.

10. Western States 100 Mile Endurance Run:
   Squaw Valley, California

Date: June 25, 1994
My age: 32
Distance: 100 miles
Time: 22:13:20
Place: 31st
Finishers: 249

Notes: As I gained more experience, I performed better in the 100-mile events. I knew what to expect. I paced myself better. I learned tricks about what to put in drop bags, the food to eat, and what size shoes to wear, as feet swell. I hydrated more effectively. Volunteers crewed for me. I had a pacer at night. These factors coupled with my better training methods led to improved performance, as did experiencing a trail for the second time.

My time was well under the 24-hour cutoff for the prestigious Cougar belt buckle. It's a fast time for someone residing at sea level. It's my best ever in a 100 miler.

11. <u>Mountain Masochist Trail Run:</u>
Blue Ridge Parkway, Virginia

Date: October 22, 1994
My age: 33
Distance: 50 miles
Time: 7:51:00 (approximate)
Place: 6th
Finishers: 155 (approximate)

Notes: I returned to David Horton's race. Fish and I drove from New England to Virginia. I ran fast over the mountainous course, which has an elevation gain of 9,200 feet. With two miles to go, I glanced back and saw a runner far behind me. The gap seemed insurmountable. Having put in so much effort, I vowed no one would pass me in the final stretch. With heavy legs from all the ups and downs, I kept pushing for the line. I emptied the tank.

With a mile to go, when I checked again, the trailing runner approached. I gave everything. He came closer. My chest heaved. I glanced back. He was sprinting and gaining ground. At the tape, I leaned. Oh, no! I edged the runner. He was flying. I sighed. It was Mike Morton. He smiled and said: "I almost caught you." I said: "Yeah, you almost did, Mike. Wow!"

Mike is a US Army Special Forces soldier. He's a winner and former record holder at the Western States 100. He also holds the US record for the 24-hour run, totaling 172 miles. Mike wasn't going to fade. If the race had been a foot longer, he would have beaten me. I had a good race. I'm sure Mike went through some bad patches. It felt nice to come out with a victory over one of the best ultra-runners of all-time.

Fish had a good race and finished well within the time limit. On our drive home, we stopped to buy gas at a self-service station. We struggled to get out of the vehicle. When we arrived home, we walked around like penguins. It would be several more days before we were walking normally. Mike made me pay.

12. <u>71st Comrades Marathon:</u>
Durban to Pietermaritzburg (up), South Africa

Date: June 17, 1996
My age: 34
Distance: 86.7K
Time: 7:38:51
Place: 1,029th
Finishers: 11,264

Notes: When apartheid ended in South Africa in 1994, the great Comrades Marathon opened to foreign runners. Tarman and I entered. It's the largest ultra-marathon in the world and steeped in tradition. I wanted to break seven hours and 30 minutes to win the coveted silver medal. I arrived at the race in excellent shape. On race day Tarman and I reached the starting line early, but the road was mobbed. We couldn't squeeze in anywhere, as competitors had slept out all night to secure their starting positions. As a result, we headed to the back.

In the first part of the race, I was frustrated that I couldn't run my own pace. I passed thousands of runners. Due to the crowds, I lost ten minutes and burned lots of unnecessary energy. I was capable of earning the silver medal, but I missed out by nine minutes. I felt disappointed. Seeing Nelson Mandela and Tarman at the finish line went some way toward making me feel better. I vowed to return and earn the silver medal. Although I qualified as a "seeded" runner, I wasn't aware of this possibility. I wouldn't make the same mistake in my second Comrades.

Tarman and I celebrated the Comrades by sharing a gigantic plateful of meat and many beers. We drove to Kruger National Park. We hobbled around gawking at animals. We prayed nothing chased us. I won't forget being taken into custody in Swaziland for not wearing seatbelts. The King's decisions are final in that country. There are no appeals. The entire trip was an adventure. We felt glad to arrive back on US soil.

13. <u>34th JFK 50:</u>
Boonsboro, Maryland

Date: November 23, 1996
My age: 35
Distance: 50.2 miles
Time: 6:46:20
Place: 16th
Finishers: 625

Notes: I ran much of the race with Ian Torrence, who became a top-notch ultra-runner, and Chris Gibbons, a multiple-time winner. We ran well together and chatted. Around mile 38 I bonked. While my companions forged ahead, I stopped at an aid station. A volunteer handed me small packets and said: "Eat these." This was my first experience with gels. They were brand new to the market. I ate three. The caffeine and calories gave me a rush. With my new-found energy, I caught Chris and Ian.

Chris said: "We never thought we'd see you again." I said: "Yeah, I didn't think you would either." We laughed. I told them about the miracle gels. We ran hard. Chris was strong and toward the end, he pulled away. I finished ahead of Ian. I ran a good race at one of the most competitive US ultras.

14. <u>Wasatch Front 100:</u>
East Layton, Utah

Date: September 6, 1997

My age: 36

Distance: 100 miles

Time: DNF, dropped out at Upper Big Water, 59.2 miles in 13:15:00

Finishers: 118

Notes: My preparation went remarkably well in the buildup. I was in the best climbing shape of my life. I trained on a StairMaster Stepmill at the highest level for a couple hours at a pop. I stacked up eight bottles of Gatorade next to the machine, and during my workout, I drank them all. Gym rats gathered to watch. They shook their heads. After each workout the staff squeegeed the large puddle from my effort. I threw multiple towels in the laundry bin. I left the gym with a spring in my step and a smile on my face.

For my attempt at Wasatch, I assembled a strong crew. Unfortunately, a few days before the race, I caught a terrible cold. I made the mistake of holding a friend's sick baby. I shouldn't have raced at all, but with my crew coming in from all over the world, I decided to give it my best shot. Due to my nasal congestion, coughing, and sore lungs, at high altitude I had trouble breathing. Despite this, I made good time. I had 41 miles to go in 23 hours, as there's a 36-hour cutoff. If healthy, I could have walked.

After months of planning and training, feeling distraught, I dropped out at mile 59.2 at Upper Bigwater with a split time of 13:15:00. A couple pacers never got a chance to run. They shared my pain. I cried. Tarman tried to console me. Dropping out felt like a major failure. At the time it meant more to me than just quitting a race. The extenuating circumstances didn't matter.

In hindsight due to my illness, I wasn't capable of finishing. I gave it my all and went deeper than I should have. Luckily, I didn't do any permanent damage to my lungs. I vowed to return.

15. Sunmart Texas Trail 50:

Huntsville, Texas

Date: December 13, 1997

My age: 36
Distance: 50.2 miles
Time: 6:27:05
Place: 7th
Finishers: 253

Notes: This run is my fastest 50 miler. I averaged 7:42 pace per mile on the trails. I was up against a strong field and went full gas the entire way. My previous ultras contributed to my mental toughness. It was another great trip to Texas.

16. US National 100K Championships:
Pittsburgh, Pennsylvania

Date: March 30, 1998
My age: 36
Distance: 100K
Time: 8:20:43
Split for 50 miles: 6:31
Place: 10th
Finishers: 75

Notes: The best ultra-runners in the USA assembled for the national championships. In hot, humid conditions, we ran a hilly loop course in the city. I ran the entire way with no walking and averaged 8:02 pace per mile. My split time was close to my best for 50 miles. Ian finished just ahead of me. I won $100, as the top-ten runners received prize money. It covered my entry fee. I didn't quit my day job.

17. Sunmart Texas Trail 50:
Huntsville, Texas

Date: December 12, 1998
My age: 37
Distance: 50.2 miles

Time: 7:37:59
Place: 27th
Finishers: 269

Notes: I came back for my fifth Texas Trail 50 in eight years. In warm conditions I ran 20 minutes slower than I had in my debut. At the time I didn't realize this would be my last Texas Trail 50.

18. Laugavegurinn 55K:
Landmannalaugar, Iceland

Date: July 24, 1999
My age: 37
Distance: 55K
Time: 5:20:15
Place: 4th
Finishers: 86

Notes: While living in Iceland, I learned about this race. I trained hard. Going into the start, I was one of the favorites. The cross-country run traverses obsidian fields, glaciers, sandy stretches, rocky areas, valleys, and mountains. It skirts nasty smelling sulfur vents that disrupt one's breathing and block vision completely. The race includes river fords in deep, fast-moving, ice-cold water. At the crossings the glacial runoff causes leg cramps. My shoes filled with silt, resulting in blisters.

The remote course wasn't well-marked. When I was leading, I got lost several times. Nevertheless, I managed fourth place and broke the previous course record. In the beautiful, rugged scenery of the interior of Iceland, I enjoyed a nice post-race party. We crossed 25 rivers to exit the interior.

19. Wasatch Front 100:
East Layton, Utah

Date: September 11-12, 1999

My age: 38
Distance: 100 miles
Time: 29:25
Place: 37th
Finishers: 114

Notes: I was determined to redeem myself at the Wasatch Front 100, referred to as "One Hundred Miles of Heaven and Hell." Although not as fit as during my previous attempt, this time I wasn't sick. I finished well within the 36-hour cutoff. When I crossed the line, I remember the race director asking: "You enjoyed that didn't you?" I nodded. I managed a smile. I avoided letting my feet do the talking. He understood and waved.

In addition to nine miles of elevation change, a portion of the race is run on animal-track trails. My legs got scratched to hell. Route finding was difficult. The footing was rough. The rugged scenery was heavenly. The air was fresh and clean. The course lived up to its billing. I felt happy to have finished one of the hardest runs in the world.

20. <u>75th Comrades Marathon:</u>
Durban to Pietermaritzburg (up), South Africa

Date: June 16, 2000
My age: 38
Distance: 87.6K
Time: 7:23:47
Place: 573th
Finishers: 20,000 (approximate)

Notes: This time I made the long journey to South Africa without Tarman. Again I raced the uphill version. The race is a point-to-point course that alternates direction each year. The down years go from Pietermaritzburg to Durban. By entering the race as a seeded, foreign runner, I secured a good starting-line position. Early on I settled into my pace.

Unfortunately, I suffered terrible diarrhea, as my stomach couldn't handle the drinking water provided at the aid stations. When I stopped roadside to go number two and dropped my shorts, groups of children giggled and pointed at my white butt. A mile later I rejoined the runners whom I'd been running alongside. Throughout the entire race, this process repeated itself many times. I didn't look forward to the sequels. I made a lot of kids smile.

My diarrhea caused chaffing and weakened me, plus because of frequent stops, it resulted in a substantial-time loss. I was determined to win the silver medal for breaking seven hours and 30 minutes. I pushed hard and ran all the famous, steep hills. I passed many walkers. At this race the most competitive ultra-marathon in the world, on a day when I was sick, I finished in the top-three percent. It was a great mental effort. I earned the silver medal.

Both my runs at Comrades were uphill. Durban is at sea level, while Pietermaritzburg sits at 2,000 feet. Along the route there are five major hills; some are two miles long with average gradients of 7%. I felt fortunate to be one of the first Americans to run Comrades and earn a silver medal. It's actually the smallest medal that I've ever won. It's the same size as a US half dollar. The medal carries a big meaning.

At the finish line, I'll never forget hearing: "Way to go, big guy!" I looked around. The person shouting *was* talking to me. The guys finishing near me all looked like the prototypical, zipper-thin, African, Olympic-quality runner. Although emaciated from diarrhea after this 54.3-mile run, more than a double marathon, I was by far the biggest person who won a silver medal. I'm 5' 10" tall and weighed 157 pounds. Everyone else whom I saw around me weighed less than 120 pounds.

The Comrades Marathon, named for fallen comrades in World War I, with its atmosphere, quality field, tough course, and great crowds is a race that I won't ever forget. In addition to its many great traditions, Comrades has a Wall of Honor. Along the course itself, there's a rock wall housing plaques with runners' names on them. In memory of our Comrades Marathon runs, Tarman and I have plaques there. I hope that we can visit our plaques someday.

21. Angeles Crest 100 Mile Endurance Run:
    Wrightwood, California

    Date: September 30, 2000
    My age: 39
    Distance: 100 miles
    Time: 27:18:40
    Place: 38th
    Finishers: 108

    Notes: This time rather than trying to win the race, I tried to finish. Although on a sub-24 hour pace until late in the race, I faded (as most do on this course) and was unable to break 24. I received the 30-hour belt buckle. It was a good performance, and I was happy to finish. I had a crew. They helped me tremendously.

22. Strolling Jim 40:
    Wartrace, Tennessee

    Date: May 4, 2002
    My age: 40
    Distance: 41.2 miles
    Time: 5:22:26
    Place: 6th
    Finishers: 60

    Notes: The founder of the Strolling Jim 40 is an eccentric named Gary Cantrell. He's also the founder of the Barkley Marathons, which fortunately, I never had a desire to run. The 40 miler is named after a Tennessee walking horse. Tarman and I competed together. Traveling from out of state, we misjudged our arrival, getting there only minutes before the gun would be fired.

Tarman and I weren't planning to warm up much anyway, but it was only on arrival that we learned there were no aid stations. There would be water jugs roadside in a few spots, but no calories. Tarman had a couple of energy bars, but I didn't have any nourishment. We tried to purchase food at a near-by shop, but they only sold guns, ammunition, and targets. I stuffed ten dollars into my shorts. In the heat, humidity, and hills, we were in for a tough day.

I ran with the front runners for most of the day, but by the marathon distance, I started to bonk. I saw a store a hundred yards off the course and ran to it, while my competitors continued. They waved. I smiled. Most of them were wise enough to bring a crew and were getting serviced regularly. For Tarman and me, we were running in our first Gary Cantrell race and didn't know what to expect. We learned.

At the store I picked up two quarts of Gatorade, but there was a line to pay. I handed my ten-dollar bill to the fellow in front of me and said: "Please pay for these." By the time I left the store, I'd drank one quart. The other disappeared a minute later. With a stomach sloshing, I ran hard. My pit stop cost me several minutes. I never saw the leaders again.

Exhausted and bonked, after finishing, I sat down with a huge plate of barbecue chicken with all the fixin's. I gorged. A familiar face approached. It wasn't Tarman. It was the fellow from the store, where I got the Gatorade. He reached out: "Here's your change. Oh, and by the way, the store owner ran out after you, thinking you were stealing. I told him you gave me the money to pay." I said: "Thanks a million." I smiled. We shook hands.

I couldn't believe the kindness the stranger had shown. He drove 15 miles to bring me my change and had defended me from the store's owner. There are many friendly people in the South. The man's gesture left me with a great impression of Tennessee. Tarman ran a solid race and arrived shortly after I finished eating.

After Tarman ate his fill, we decided to tour the Jack Daniels Distillery, which is in the dry county of Lynchburg. At the start of the tour, the guide warned that the tour involved hundreds of

steps. We just smiled at each other. A few obese people bailed. Tarman and I hobbled up and down steps for an hour. We were
"forced" to buy Gold Label, as they're only allowed to sell collec-
tor's items in the dry county.

For my next attempt at the Strolling Jim, I planned to arrive
with a support crew and my own bottle of JD for the post-race
celebration.

23. Nifty 50, New England Championships:
Coventry, Rhode Island

Date: November 17, 2002
My age: 41
Distance: 50 miles
Time: 6:55:55
Place: 4th

Notes: My Mom and family members came to see me race on home
soil. I went out fast with the goal of setting a new personal best
for 50 miles. The rolling hills took a toll, as did the chilly weather,
and I struggled at the end. With my Mom and family cheering me
on, I hung on for fourth place. This was the last time my Mom saw
me run. I wish I could have won. I just missed the podium.

24. Strolling Jim 40:
Wartrace, Tennessee

Date: May 1, 2004
My age: 42
Distance: 41.2 miles
Time: 5:28:25
Place: 5th
Finishers: 60

Notes: I returned to the Strolling Jim with Tarman and Ironwoman,
who would crew for us. We arrived at the starting line with plenty

of time to spare, and this time we were wiser. I started well and was running near the leaders. I opened a sizeable gap on Tarman, which I knew meant that Ironwoman would have trouble servicing us both. When I did see her, I took in calories and fluids.

About 20 miles into the race, in the backroads of Tennessee, a dangerous-looking dog ran toward me. Zeus seemed a third Pit-bull, Boxer, and Rottweiler. He had big teeth, which he liked to show me. Zeus kept darting back-and-forth beside me, and I worried that he would take a chunk out of my leg. I worried until I became so trashed that I didn't care if Zeus bit me. He would be doing me a favor. Eventually, I understood Zeus was harmless, friendly, and just wanted to run. And, run he did. Zeus ran all the way to the finish line with me.

When we reached the end, we were both ravenous. I fixed my-self a huge plate of Southern BBQ, while Zeus went around con-suming any food that people had left unattended. A spectator shouted: "I recognize that dog!" I said: "He followed me for the last 20 miles." Another person offered: "I'm going to return him." Again I was amazed at the kindness of the people in the South. I rubbed Zeus's full stomach one-final time. He wagged his tail, showed me his teeth, and departed for home in the back of a pickup.

When Tarman finished, we went to the gun shop. He pur-chased targets with Osama bin Laden's face in the bullseye. The rolling green hills of Tennessee in horse country and the friendly low-key atmosphere of the race made it one of my all-time favor-ites. Gary knows how to put on an ultra. Many of the all-time greats have competed in this race, including Andy Jones, who still holds the astonishing course record of 3:59:26. This record is un-der six minutes per mile pace on a hilly course that includes "The Walls." In my best effort on the course, I ran a 7:40 pace if I deduct the time spent in the store.

25. Tussey Mountain 50, US National Championships:
State College, Pennsylvania

Date: October 16, 2010
My age: 49
Distance: 50 miles
Time: 7:41:17
Overall: 14th
Age group: 3rd

Notes: At the early morning start, the race director shouted: "For how many of you is this your first ultra?" Many hands went up and newbies shouted excitedly. People clapped. Things quieted down, and I shouted: "For how many of you is this your last ultra?" My hand shot up. Everyone laughed. I smiled. To date, I don't have plans to race another ultra. I do occasionally go out for a training run over 50K.

I didn't finish three of the 100-mile races that I entered, but in those cases I dropped out at 59, 61, and 76 miles. So in a way, they were ultras as well. They were harder efforts than my 50 milers. My feet often decided how well I ran in ultras. I competed before the trail-running shoe had been invented, and my feet would have benefited from more support. Given the limitations of my feet, I ran best at the 50-mile and 100K distances.

Now I train in Salomon trail runners, which offer far more support than my previous racing shoes. Shoe technology helped improve performances on the track and roads. It has impacted trail performances over the ultra-distance even more. Good trail-running shoes would have saved me a tremendous amount of suffering. In some races I'm sure that I could have reduced the amount of walking that I did if better shoes had been available. Although my times would have been much faster, I probably wouldn't have improved my placing much, as others would have derived similar benefits.

7. Marathons

"I'm okay, Mom."

I competed in 55 marathon races. Before listing those runs, I present a few facts. My fastest marathon was at the Tucson Marathon in 2005, where at the age of 44, I ran a 2:51:45. When age-graded, that equates to a 2:41:15. I went the marathon distance or farther 584 times. I ran 15 sub-three hour marathons. When age-graded, I ran 25 sub-three hour marathons. The average time of my ten best marathons is 2:53:31. The average time of my ten best age-graded marathons is 2:49:19, which suggests that I got better with age. Note that I had five age-graded performances under 2:50.

The average time of my 33 best marathons is 2:59:53. The average time of my 45 best age-graded marathons is 2:59:45. When you consider my trail marathons and the hot marathons in Thailand, my average performance on a "reasonable" course, when age-graded, was sub-three hours. The average time of my best seven Boston Marathons is 2:57:53. The average age-graded time of my ten Boston Marathons is 2:58:53, and one of them took place the day after the London Marathon. If I remove it, my average age-graded time drops to 2:57:17.

It was only in the process of writing this book that I noticed I had a 24-year streak in which I ran a marathon race every year. If I'd known that, I would have kept the streak alive. I ran the marathon distance or farther in training for 32 of the past 33 years. When I took an around-the-world trip in 2019, I missed one year. My 30-year streak ended. I never thought about it until now. Many runners use streaks to stay motivated. Some run every day for a minimum distance, say three miles, year after year. I knew a guy who left his hospital bed to keep a 25-year streak alive.

I won one marathon overall—the Low Country Distance Classic Marathon in 2004 in South Carolina. I won several races in the Masters category. My Masters wins are as follows:

- Low Country Distance Classic Marathon 2003
- Atlanta Marathon 2003
- Bay State Marathon 2004 (1st 40-49)
- Low Country Distance Classic Marathon 2004
- Rutledge Marathon 2009 (1st 45-49)

I finished in the top-ten overall at the following marathons:

- 10th Cape Cod Marathon 1993
- 5th Nipmuck Trail Marathon 1994
- 10th Nipmuck Trail Marathon 1997
- 3rd Tybee Marathon 1999
- 5th Myvatn Marathon 1999
- 7th Leadville Trail Marathon 2001
- 6th Tybee Marathon 2003
- 2nd Low Country Distance Classic Marathon 2003
- 5th Atlanta Marathon 2003
- 9th Bay State Marathon 2004
- 1st Low Country Distance Classic Marathon 2004
- 10th Phuket Marathon 2006
- 6th Chiang Mai Marathon 2008
- 4th Rutledge Marathon 2009

In many other marathons, I finished in the top ten in the Masters division. My most frequently run marathons are the Boston Marathon (ten times), the Tybee Marathon (six times), the Nipmuck Trail Marathon (five times), and the Phuket Marathon (four times). I tried to find good races nearby where I was living and support them. In nearly all races I ran as hard as possible. The exceptions were times when I was using a race as a training run. Of course, over my marathon career and with a focus on other sports, I didn't always enter races with the same level of running fitness. With this background I list my marathons.

1. Rhode Island Marathon:
   Newport, Rhode Island

   Date: October 22, 1989
   My age: 28
   Distance: 26.2 miles
   Time: 3:23:06
   Age-graded time: 3:23:06
   Place: 216th
   Finishers: 1,200 (approximate)

   Notes: My Mom and Dad were there. My Mom cried because I was hurting so badly. After that, I don't think she wanted to come see me run. It was too painful. Although I hadn't trained too much, I pushed the pace hard. I ran the entire race. In the later stages, I passed many competitors who were walking.

2. Nipmuck Trail Marathon:
   Ashford, Connecticut

   Date: June 10, 1990
   My age: 28
   Distance: 26 miles (approximate)
   Time: 3:54:00
   Age-graded time: 3:54:00
   Place: 15th
   Finishers: 85 (approximate)

   Notes: I fell in love with this low-key race. The aid stations were spotty clusters of self-service water jugs, sitting near the trail. We needed to jump over several fences. The trail is challenging and beautiful. The best trail runners in New England show up at this race.

3. Cape Cod Marathon:
   Falmouth, Massachusetts

   Date: October 28, 1990
   My age: 29
   Distance: 26.2 miles
   Time: 3:03:36
   Age-graded time: 3:03:36
   Place: 78th
   Finishers: 471

   Notes: I took 20 minutes off the time from my first marathon. I ran a seven-minute pace, and I came close to breaking three hours. Every time I visit Cape Cod, I think back to Fish's and my epic double century, completed as young teenagers. This trip brought back lots of good memories.

4. Cape Cod Marathon:
   Falmouth, Massachusetts

   Date: October 27, 1991
   My age: 30
   Distance: 26.2 miles
   Time: 3:00:52
   Age-graded time: 3:00:52
   Place: 45th
   Finishers: 366

   Notes: I tried to break three hours, but failed. If I stayed healthy, I sensed that I would soon break three hours on the roads.

5. Nipmuck Trail Marathon:
   Ashford, Connecticut

   Date: June 7, 1992

My age: 30
Distance: 26 miles (approximate)
Time: 3:56:53
Age-graded time: 3:56:53
Place: 13th
Finishers: 88

Notes: I had another good time at the Nipmuck.

6. Maine Marathon:
    Portland, Maine

    Date: October 4, 1992
    My age: 31
    Distance: 26.2 miles
    Time: 2:54:22
    Age-graded time: 2:54:22
    Place: 20th (approximate)
    Finishers: 400 (approximate)

    Notes: I broke three hours for the first time, taking six minutes off my previous best. Unfortunately, I would never do that again. This was my fourth road marathon, and I improved in each race.

7. Cape Cod Marathon:
    Hyannis, Massachusetts

    Date: March 7, 1993
    My age: 31
    Distance: 26.2 miles
    Time: 2:53:31
    Age-graded time: 2:53:31
    Place: 10th
    Finishers: 500 (approximate)

Notes: I set a new PR. I continued lowering it at each race. I thought I would soon break 2:40.

8. Nipmuck Trail Marathon:
    Ashford, Connecticut

    Date: June 6, 1993
    My age: 31
    Distance: 26 miles (approximate)
    Time: 3:37:15
    Age-graded time: 3:37:15
    Place: 12th
    Finishers: 123

    Notes: This was a solid run on the tough, rocky course. It equated to a sub-three hour road marathon.

9. Rhode Island Marathon:
    Providence, Rhode Island

    Date: November 7, 1993
    My age: 32
    Distance: 26.2 miles
    Time: 3:01:49
    Age-graded time: 3:01:49
    Place: 73rd
    Finishers: 676

    Notes: This marathon was the first road marathon where I didn't improve my time. The reason was because I'd run in a 100-mile ultra-marathon race three weeks earlier, and my legs hadn't recovered. Although I went out fast on home soil, my fatigue from over racing caught up to me.

10. Boston Marathon:
    Hopkinton, Massachusetts

Date: April 18, 1994
My age: 32
Distance: 26.2 miles
Time: 2:52:25
Age-graded time: 2:52:25
Place: 684th
Finishers: 8,105

Notes: I grew up just south of Boston, and this race is important to me. All serious marathoners from the East Coast dream of running in the Boston Marathon, as do many runners from around the world. This race took place when the Boston Marathon was still a relatively small and exclusive marathon. The qualifying times are rigorous, so it's considered an elite marathon. I ran a new best time. I felt like a sub-2:50 would soon be in the cards, but with my focus on ultras, it never happened.

11. <u>Burlington Marathon:</u>
    Burlington, Vermont

    Date: May 29, 1994
    My age: 32
    Distance: 26.2 miles
    Time: 2:54:04
    Age-graded time: 2:54:04
    Place: 46th
    Finishers: 966

    Notes: The course is beautiful. I often finished in the top-five percent of my races, as I did here.

12. <u>Nipmuck Trail Marathon:</u>
    Ashford, Connecticut

    Date: June 5, 1994

My age: 32
Distance: 26 miles (approximate)
Time: 3:24:11
Age-graded time: 3:24:11
Place: 5th
Finishers: 120

Notes: This was a great run and an excellent time on this difficult, hilly course. I felt strong the entire way and finished 5th against a quality field. This race was one of my best runs. In my mind, it equated to a 2:46 road marathon.

13. <u>Boston Marathon:</u>
    Hopkinton, Massachusetts

    Date: April 17, 1995
    My age: 33
    Distance: 26.2 miles
    Time: 2:52:01
    Age-graded time: 2:52:01
    Place: 530th
    Finishers: 8,259

    Notes: I improved on my previous time at Boston by 24 seconds. This is my fastest Boston. I set a new PR, too.

14. <u>Marathon Popular de Valencia (Compensada):</u>
    Valencia, Spain

    Date: February 4, 1996
    My age: 34
    Distance: 26.2 miles
    Time: 2:58:21
    Age-graded time: 2:58:21
    Place: 309th
    Finishers: 1,500

Notes: While on sabbatical for a year in Barcelona, I ran this race. I was inspired by the great runners in my New Hampshire neighborhood—Cathy O'Brien and Lynn Jennings—who both competed in the Barcelona Olympics. The format featured delayed starting times, based on your age and gender. Since I was a young male, I started in the final group. I enjoyed this format because there were runners whom you could key off throughout.

There were only three aid stations in the race. It was a hot day. At one aid station, I grabbed a big bottle that the volunteers were using to fill up small cups. Someone shouted at me in Spanish (the equivalent of): "Don't take that!" The guy chased me. He caught me, as I finished the last sip. I said: "Gracias," while passing him back the empty. He shook his finger. I smiled. I ran.

Overall placing wasn't adjusted for time. I managed to finish in about the top 20% despite having the latest starting time. Although I wasn't training as much in Barcelona, as I had been in the states, my residual fitness from my thru-hike of the Appalachian Trail served me well.

At the finish line, a volunteer handed me a bag of Valencia oranges. I was too cramped and exhausted to take advantage of the free massage. I didn't have sufficient energy to carry the oranges around either. I'd walked a few miles to reach the starting line, and I needed to walk back to reach my hotel. It made for another ultra.

15. XIX Catalunya Marathon:
    Barcelona, Spain

Date: March 17, 1996
My age: 34
Distance: 26.2 miles
Time: 3:05:06
Age-graded time: 3:05:06
Place: 340th
Finishers: 3,000 (approximate)

Notes: It was fun to run the 1992 course from the Barcelona Olympics. While cheering roadside, it seemed all spectators were smoking. I remember "An-e-mal!" being shouted. Completing the final 400 meters in the Olympic stadium to a huge, enthusiastic crowd thrilled me, even though the packed stadium existed only in my mind. I heard the same cheers that Cathy and Lynn had received. In reality there were about 2,500 fans.

16. Bay State Marathon:
    Lowell, Massachusetts

    Date: October 13, 1996
    My age: 35
    Distance: 26.2 miles
    Time: 2:53:46
    Age-graded time: 2:53:46
    Place: 18th
    Finishers: 711

    Notes: My Mom came to this race, and I wanted to perform well. I ran a good race, finishing in the top 2.5%. In marathons taking place around Boston, there are lots of good runners, as they prepare and try to qualify for the Boston Marathon.

17. Boston Marathon:
    Hopkinton, Massachusetts

    Date: April 21, 1997
    My age: 35
    Distance: 26.2 miles
    Time: 2:59:22
    Age-graded time: 2:59:22
    Place: 770th
    Finishers: 8,910

Notes: This race was another Boston Marathon where I needed to sprint down Boylston Street to break three hours. By now I had the starting logistics in Hopkinton pretty well mastered.

18. Nipmuck Trail Marathon:
Ashford, Connecticut

Date: June 1, 1997
My age: 35
Distance: 26 miles (approximate)
Time: 3:41:40
Age-graded time: 3:41:40
Place: 10th
Finishers: 120

Notes: I usually drove from New Hampshire to run this race. On this morning I had a flat tire on my car. This added stress to my morning routine. I ran another solid race at the challenging, competitive Nipmuck. From my previous trips, I knew some of the runners. It was fun to catch up with them and share our enthusiasm for trail running.

19. Boston Marathon:
Hopkinton, Massachusetts

Date: April 20, 1998
My age: 36
Distance: 26.2 miles
Time: 3:01:12
Age-graded time: 3:01:01
Place: 1,120th
Finishers: 10,307

Notes: Although I gave it my best, I was disappointed not to break three hours. Running fast up Heartbreak Hill had taken a little too much out of me.

20. Tybee Marathon:
    Tybee Island, Georgia

    Date: February 13, 1999
    My age: 37
    Distance: 26.2 miles
    Time: 2:54:26
    Age-graded time: 2:53:44
    Place: 3rd
    Finishers: 181

    Notes: I ran an excellent race in hot and humid conditions. At one
    point I thought I might win. I pushed all the way to the finish, but
    the winner maintained his pace. This was one of the few marathons
    where I finished on the podium.

21. Boston Marathon:
    Hopkinton, Massachusetts

    Date: April 19, 1999
    My age: 37
    Distance: 26.2 miles
    Time: 2:58:04
    Age-graded time: 2:57:21
    Place: 468th
    Finishers: 11,293

    Notes: Although the Boston Marathon was becoming more popular
    each year, due to the qualification standards, they maintained a
    high-quality field. I paced myself well up Heartbreak Hill. I finished
    in around the top-four percent, which is a respectable showing
    when you consider that one percent of the runners are profession-
    als. After a near miss the previous year, I dipped under three hours.

22. Myvatn Marathon:

Myvatn, Iceland

Date: June 25, 1999
My age: 37
Distance: 26.2 miles
Time: 2:55:26
Age-graded time: 2:54:44
Place: 5th
Finishers: 66

Notes: This run was a midnight marathon, meaning the race started at 12 AM. Iceland sits far north, so it wasn't completely dark around the time of the summer solstice. Myvatn means mosquito in Icelandic. This race is the mosquito-lake marathon. I carried mosquito netting, as we ran around the lake. I was in great shape, and I ran an excellent race, pushing hard throughout the entire rolling route. When we encountered strong headwinds, another competitor and I shared pacing duties. Needless to say, I was exhausted while finishing at 3:00 AM.

23. Tybee Marathon:
Tybee Island, Georgia

Date: February 5, 2000
My age: 38
Distance: 26.2 miles
Time: 3:05:20
Age-graded time: 3:03:40
Place: 17th
Finishers: 169

Notes: I used this event as a training run to prepare for the Boston Marathon.

24. Boston Marathon:
Hopkinton, Massachusetts

Date: April 17, 2000
My age: 38
Distance: 26.2 miles
Time: 3:00:52
Age-graded time: 2:59:14
Place: 1,357th
Finishers: 15,663

Notes: I felt disappointed not to break three hours. It was always a pleasure to come back and run Boston, especially with the tremendous crowd support at Wellesley College. High fiving and kissing the girls often drained more energy than it injected. I loved their screaming. In hindsight I wouldn't have done things differently. Tarman continued to extend his streak of consecutive Boston Marathons, and we traveled to and from the race together.

25. Leadville Trail Marathon:
    Leadville, Colorado

Date: July 7, 2001
My age: 39
Distance: 26.2 miles
Time: 4:30:29
Age-graded time: 4:26:09
Place: 7th
Finishers: 128

Notes: While out drinking margaritas in Leadville, I met a group of runners. They informed me that the next day they were running the Leadville Trail Marathon. They weren't drinking. I asked if I could sign up, and they said: "Yes." Although they doubted I would run, I showed up the next day. I ran a great race, having carboloaded on my favorite frozen beverage. The group reunited at the finish and laughed. The time is slow, but the lowest elevation of the mountainous race is 9,300 feet.

26. Tybee Marathon:
    Tybee Island, Georgia

    Date: February 2, 2002
    My age: 40
    Distance: 26.2 miles
    Time: 3:09:50
    Age-graded time: 3:05:16
    Place: 14th
    Masters: 7th
    Finishers: 233

    Notes: Whether or not I was in my best shape, it became a tradition to run this race.

27. Tybee Marathon:
    Tybee Island, Georgia

    Date: February 1, 2003
    My age: 41
    Distance: 26.2 miles
    Time: 2:56:37
    Age-graded time: 2:50:57
    Place: 6th
    Masters: 2nd
    Finishers: 318

    Notes: I ran another solid Tybee and finished in the top-two percent. Although run during the Savannah winter, the race was often hot and humid. It was always a satisfying accomplishment to break three hours. This run was part of my buildup for the PCT hike.

28. Bluffton Low Country Distance Classic:
    Bluffton, South Carolina

Date: October 26, 2003
My age: 42
Distance: 26.2 miles
Time: 3:12:56
Age-graded time: 3:05:12
Place: 2nd
Masters: 1st
Finishers: 50

Notes: I ran a good race, and almost took the overall win in hot and humid conditions. I sensed that I might win this race in the future. I won the Masters division. I was on the overall podium. I completed this race with very little run training and relied on the residual fitness from my PCT hike.

29. Atlanta Marathon:
    Atlanta, Georgia

Date: November 27, 2003
My age: 42
Distance: 26.2 miles
Time: 2:54:55
Age-graded time: 2:47:54
Place: 6th
Masters: 1st
Finishers: 644

Notes: This race marked one of my best performances. I negative split the course. It has lots of rolling hills. It was hot and humid. At the halfway point, I was in 18th. Then in rapid succession, I heard: "You're in 15th," "You're in 12th," "You're in 10th," and "You're in 8th," … I thought: "I can win this."

I ran faster as the race progressed, and at the end I was flying. If the race had been 50K instead of 42.2K, I might have won. My strength carried over from the PCT. At a big-city marathon such as Atlanta, it felt good to win the Masters division. In front of a huge crowd, I received a nice award—a blanket with lettering—on the podium. Because it was Thanksgiving Day, I celebrated with a giant post-race meal.

30. Boston Marathon:
Hopkinton, Massachusetts

Date: April 19, 2004
My age: 42
Distance: 26.2 miles
Time: 3:01:12
Age-graded time: 2:53:56
Place: 353rd
Masters: 69th/3,877
Starters: 16,743

Notes: With a temperature of 85°F at the start, this run was one of the hottest Boston Marathons on record! I finished in about the top-two percent. Considering one percent of the runners were professionals, this race was one of my all-time best. I still carried fitness from my PCT hike. I had a solid placing in the Masters division. The heat alone kept me from breaking three hours, but I was close. My age-graded time of 2:53:56 in the heat was solid.

31. Bay State Marathon:
Lowell, Massachusetts

Date: October 17, 2004
My age: 43
Distance: 26.2 miles
Time: 2:54:00
Age-graded time: 2:45:38
Place: 9th
Masters: 2nd
Finishers: 497

Notes: I ran an excellent race and finished in the top ten. I was on a streak of good marathons, which related to my strength from setting the FKT on the PCT. My age-graded time of 2:45:38 was one of my best. My confidence grew.

32. Bluffton Low Country Distance Classic:
Bluffton, South Carolina

Date: October 31, 2004
My age: 43
Distance: 26.2 miles
Time: 3:02:49
Age-graded time: 2:54:01
Place: 1st
Masters: 1st
Finishers: 49

Notes: With temperatures near 100°F and the heat index well over 120°F, this race was one of my best. Many runners didn't start due to the heat, and other runners dropped out along the way. At about mile ten, I needed to go "number two" in the wild. I ran into the "bushes." I wasn't carrying toilet paper. I did my business as fast as possible, but I lost a couple minutes.

When I stopped, there were a few runners ahead of me. I learned they were running the half marathon, not the full. Half marathoners complete one circuit of the two-loop course. My running companion from before my bathroom break was now in first place. I had to catch him.

I told myself: "You can't lose this race over a bathroom break!" And: "This might be your only chance to win a marathon!" On the winding route in extreme heat, I kept a steady pace. This was my 32nd marathon race. I completed the AT; I set the FKT on the PCT; I completed many Ironman-distance triathlons; I completed 100-mile runs.

I wasn't going to lose over a bathroom break. I relied on my experience. At mile 18, I could see the lead runner again. At mile

21, while he was taking a drink, I caught up at an aid station. Despite the brutal conditions, I pushed through the aid station without refueling. I was desperately thirsty and dehydrated. But, I wanted to make a statement and gain an advantage.

I increased my pace. I was flying. Sweat poured into my eyes. The former leader caught me and was on my heels. I went full gas, as I heard his labored breathing. He grunted. I quieted my breathing. I ran tall. After one mile he dropped back. Over the remaining four miles, I emptied the tank.

The famous pitcher Satchel Paige said: "Don't look back. Something might be gaining on you." He wasn't a runner. I ignored his admonition. Every so often, I glanced back to see if anyone was gaining. In fact, during the last four miles, I stretched my lead to eight minutes over the second-place runner. Although cramping, I wasn't going to let a victory slip away. When I crossed the line in first place, it was a proud moment.

While hanging out at the finish line, I felt horrendous with nausea and heat exhaustion. A guy came up to me and said: "Did you hear some guy almost broke three in these conditions?" He shook his head back-and-forth in disbelief. "Unbelievable," he said: "I can't believe it!" I raised my head, looked him in the eye, and said: "It was me." He couldn't believe it. I managed a smile. If not for my bathroom break, I would have broken three. Like many of my races, I traveled to this event alone. So there was no one to share in my glory. I drove home with a smile and a big trophy.

33. Tybee Marathon:
Tybee Island, Georgia

Date: February 5, 2005
My age: 43
Distance: 26.2 miles
Time: 3:09:16
Age-graded time: 3:00:10
Place: 11th
Finishers: 273

Notes: I used this edition of Tybee as a training run for my upcoming, back-to-back London and Boston Marathon double. I didn't know if running these two marathons on consecutive days had ever been accomplished. In 2005 it was one of those rare occasions, when the feat was possible. Tarman would be attempting the rare double with me. My time in this race indicated that my training was on schedule.

34. London Marathon:
    London, England

Date: April 17, 2005
My age: 43
Distance: 26.2 miles
Time: 3:02:38
Age-graded time: 2:53:51
Place: 1,294th
Finishers: 35,261

Notes: The start line in London was chaos with one of the largest fields ever assembled for a marathon. There were probably 40,000+ starters. Three separate starting venues helped to spread out the field of runners. When the different groups of runners merged, it was beautiful, like the confluence of three colorful rivers mixing, with the bobbing runners providing turbulent water. In the race Paula Radcliffe set a world record for a women's only marathon, as the elite women ran separately. At one point she flew by me on the opposite side of the road, as did the world-class men's field.

I enjoyed the sights and smells, as the course traversed London's neighborhoods. I also enjoyed that I wasn't pushing the pace like I did in all my other marathons. I felt comfortable. I saved something for the next day's Boston Marathon. I dreamed of running sub-three hour races in both London and Boston. I could have broken three hours, but I backed off my pace. I ran a good, solid, steady race.

When Tarman finished, we departed from Buckingham Palace via the Tube, returned to our hotel, showered, and headed straight for the airport, to catch our flight to Boston. Tarman wanted to stay at his house in Maine, so when we got to Boston, we had a long drive ahead. Of course, we needed to drive back to Boston the next day for the start in Hopkinton. By now though, we understood the schedule required to arrive at the start on time. Due to many road closures, it took a number of years to optimize and make this process less stressful.

35. <u>Boston Marathon:</u>
Hopkinton, Massachusetts

Date: April 18, 2005
My age: 43
Distance: 26.2 miles
Time: 3:23:31
Age-graded time: 3:13:44
Place: 2,654th
Finishers: 17,549

Notes: Needless to say, after crossing the Atlantic from my run in London the day before, my legs were sore going into this race. My legs were hurting more than during the second half of a 50-mile run. They were stiff. At the Boston Marathon, runners are seeded based on entry times. A crazy number of runners passed me in the first few miles, because due to sore legs, I wasn't running my entry pace.

The first half felt painful. By the second half, I found myself passing other runners. It became apparent that I wasn't going to achieve my three-hour goal. In fact, I ran 25 seconds slower than my first-ever marathon in Rhode Island. This was the first time I'd ever run slower on the road than in my debut marathon, 16 years earlier. Given the situation, I accepted that my marathoning had come a long way.

Tarman finished his Boston Marathon in a good time as well. The double was a nice achievement for us, as it was a goal that we dreamed up on our own. The London Marathon is always run on a Sunday and the Boston Marathon always on the third Monday in April, but there are few times when the days are consecutive. That's okay with me, because I won't be doing this double again, even if the opportunity presents itself. I'm sure Tarman feels the same.

36. Tucson Marathon:
Tucson, Arizona

Date: December 5, 2005
My age: 44
Distance: 26.2 miles
Time: 2:51:45
Age-graded time: 2:41:15
Place: 18th
Age group (40-45): 3rd
Finishers: 1,045

Notes: My dream was always to run under 2:40, even though I'd never broken 2:50. Tucson is reputedly a fast course, despite its hills and elevation. Overall, the course is downhill. I came to the race in great shape. I pushed through the half marathon in a PR of 1:18:00 on pace to break 2:40. Even through 18 miles, I was on a sub-2:40. But, shortly thereafter, abdominal cramping made it hard for me to breathe.

I slowed considerably over the final miles, but I managed to run my best time by a handful of seconds. My fast split convinced me that I was capable of a sub-2:40 on the right course and day. But, it never happened. As of this writing, my age-graded time of 2:41:15 is the best of my career. Although I should have been happy with my PR and best age-graded performance ever, I felt disappointed. I could have run a 2:45 if I hadn't gone all in. I came so close to a major breakthrough.

37. ING Temple Marathon:
    Bangkok, Thailand

Date: March 19, 2006
My age: 44
Distance: 26.2 miles
Time: 3:27:04
Age-graded time: 3:15:27
Place: 20th
Finishers: 350

Notes: Like most marathons in Thailand, this one was super-hot and humid. The early start meant many barking and chasing dogs, especially for the leaders. The race was billed as a cultural event and passed by dozens of temples. It turned into a survival test.

38. Boston Marathon:
    Hopkinton, Massachusetts

Date: April 17, 2006
My age: 44
Distance: 26.2 miles
Time: 3:14:38
Age-graded time: 3:03:43
Place: 2,876th
Finishers: 19,688

Notes: One year I needed to give up my race number at the Boston Marathon to a former Japanese champion. I don't remember if it was this year or not. My research was inconclusive. But, let me relay the story here. It was quite something for a Japanese person to travel to America right after World War II. Never mind to come and win the Boston Marathon.

The Boston Athletics Association called me. They explained that my number, say 1,750, was the number worn by a former champion from Japan. He was returning to celebrate his victory and run Boston again, 50 years later. The champion requested to wear his lucky number. It was coincidence that I had been assigned the number. Of course, I immediately agreed to give it up. I was happy to become part of his story. He was a tremendous inspiration!

The numbers at Boston are seedings by time. The race start is cordoned off into corrals, and you can enter a corral only if you possess a number in the appropriate range. As a return favor, the organizers gave me an elite number, say 180. That number meant that I could start up near the professional runners. In fact, I was right behind the pros with maybe a 30-yard gap between us.

My starting position was by far the best that I'd ever had at the Boston Marathon. I was usually in the second or third corral, but this time I was at the front. My chip time would be the same as my actual time. I didn't have as good a run as I usually do at Boston. And, all throughout the day, I heard the knowledgeable fans at the side of the road saying things like: "Boy, that guy really blew up," "Look at that guy's number, how'd he end up way back here?," "How did that guy ever get such a low number?," or "He doesn't look like he could run a 2:18." Needless to say, hearing such comments for three hours did little to improve my mental state. I thought of the old Japanese champion and hoped that he'd had a better time on the course than I. I shook my head and smiled.

39. Phuket Marathon:
Phuket, Thailand

Date: June 18, 2006
My age: 44
Distance: 26.2 miles
Time: 3:35:36
Age-graded time: 3:23:30
Place: 10th

Finishers: 280

Notes: I believe this was the inaugural race. I was the first Westerner to finish on the hot, humid, and hilly course. Like many marathons in Thailand, the race started in the dark. The early morning starts mean many aggressive dogs, the inability to enjoy the scenery, and the more likelihood of getting lost. The advantage is less traffic. Mine was a solid performance and a good run. I liked traveling to Phuket for scuba diving and to visit Fiddlehead, as he'd moved there. I figured that I would run this race again at some point.

40. Pattaya Marathon:
    Pattaya, Thailand

    Date: July 15, 2007
    My age: 45
    Distance: 26.2 miles
    Time: 3:30:09
    Age-graded time: 3:16:40
    Place: 74th
    Finishers: 500

Notes: Most marathons in Thailand have 4:00 or 5:00 AM starts, to try and beat the heat. However, it actually feels hotter at that time because the humidity is higher. Once the sun comes up, the air dries out a bit. While walking to the starting line, a couple bargirls propositioned me: "Hey mister, you wanna go?" I replied: "No thanks, I'm on my way to run a marathon." One girl asked: "Short time? Up to you. He-he-he." I smiled and laughed. They were disappointed.

Many Thais have guard dogs. In the darkness the hounds chase runners. When you're near the front, you're usually running alone. The dogs haven't seen many runners yet, and they're still energetic and curious. While protecting their turf, the dogs bark like hell. In total darkness it isn't a pleasant feeling being chased by dogs. The pitter-pattering pack's paws play with your nerves. It doesn't help to improve your overall time either, since you need to make sudden bursts to avoid getting bitten.

I suffered from heat exhaustion. After the event no beverages were available. The race organizers were still ironing out basic logistics. I walked into a restaurant and grabbed three cans of soda from the refrigerator, motioning that I intended to pay. About to pass out, I lay down on the floor. I drank the sodas. Once revived, I got up from my puddle, handed a girl plenty of money, and departed without collecting my change. For several hours I kept telling myself: "If this gets any worse, you need to go to a hospital." I felt terrible for days. Tarman ran this race with me and had a similar experience.

41. Marine Corps Marathon:
    Washington, DC

    Date: October 28, 2007
    My age: 46
    Distance: 26.2 miles
    Time: 3:02:52
    Age-graded time: 2:49:40
    Place: 218th
    Age group: 17th
    Finishers: 20,667

    Notes: I wanted to run the Marine Corps Marathon to honor the US military and to see the beautiful sights of Washington, DC. I averaged a fraction under seven minutes per mile, but I wasn't able to break three hours. I managed to finish near the top 1%.

42. Tybee Marathon:
    Tybee Island, Georgia

    Date: February 2, 2008
    My age: 46
    Distance: 26.2 miles

Time: 3:24:53
Age-graded time: 3:10:05
Place: 33rd
Finishers: 317

Notes: This race was one minute slower than my first marathon, 20 years earlier.

43. Phuket Marathon:
    Phuket, Thailand

    Date: June 15, 2008
    My age: 46
    Distance: 26.2 miles
    Time: 3:22:04
    Age-graded time: 3:07:29
    Place: 12th
    Age group: 2nd
    Finishers: 400

    Notes: This run was a solid performance in the heat and humidity of Thailand. Although only three minutes faster, it was a much better run than my Tybee Marathon four months earlier.

44. Marine Corps Marathon:
    Washington, DC

    Date: October 26, 2008
    My age: 47
    Distance: 26.2 miles
    Time: 4:17:51
    Age-graded time: 3:57:10
    Place: 6,368th
    Finishers: 18,273

Notes: I was with a group of friends to honor their fallen son, who is buried at Arlington National Cemetery. We arrived late to the start. When I saw the signs reading '7:00' in the section where I was standing, I thought: "Okay, this isn't such a bad position and seven minutes per mile is about right." It turned out I was at the back of the field. The sign that I interpreted as meaning seven minutes per mile actually stood for a seven-hour marathon! That is 16 minute per mile pace! Nine minutes slower per mile than I expected to run.

I never started a race so far back. In my first Comrades Marathon, starting in a bad position had cost me a silver medal. I ran on sidewalks and lawns and passed hundreds of runners every minute. I passed about 10,000 runners. Due to road congestion, it became clear that I couldn't race. I needed to take it easy and try to enjoy the race to the extent possible. Although I was in good shape to run fast, it wasn't possible. I enjoyed the atmosphere created by the Marines. I enjoyed DC. It was my first marathon where I wasn't sore after the race.

45. Chiang Mai Marathon:
    Chiang Mai, Thailand

Date: December 28, 2008
My age: 47
Distance: 26.2 miles
Time: 3:03:10
Age-graded time: 2:47:42
Place: 6th
Age group: 3rd
Finishers: 100

Notes: I ran an excellent race. I pushed hard the entire way. With one mile to go, I caught a young Thai runner. He appeared to be about 20 years old. He looked fit and had muscular calves. I figured he was a football (soccer) player. When I passed, he sped up. I ran hard, but the young Thai had a lot left in the tank and beat me.

Later I learned there was prize money for the top-five runners. My Thai competitor really wanted/needed that 1,000 baht (about $30). I made him earn it. I had nothing left. Even if there had been a million dollars on the line, I couldn't have gone faster. For such a sum, he would have been flying.

I didn't realize this was probably the last time that I would run under seven-minute pace per mile for the marathon. A feat I accomplished in my second road marathon and most others marathons since. My focus shifted toward cycling.

46. Kentucky Derby Festival Marathon:
Louisville, Kentucky

Date: April 25, 2009
My age: 47
Distance: 26.2 miles
Time: 3:14:02
Age-graded time: 2:58:28
Place: 15th
Finishers: 1,200

Notes: The race was held a week before the Kentucky Derby. It was a shame that I couldn't stay around to watch the derby. The temperature and humidity were high. It was a solid effort, as I finished near the top-one percent. My age-graded time of 2:58:28, put me in the top ten. After the race I stayed at the Rocking Horse Inn and had a great time. When I drove there, at every block, a female voice on my GPS said: "Recalculating," with disdain, as I missed each turn. "She" hadn't been informed of the road closures due to the marathon.

47. Phuket Marathon:
Phuket, Thailand

Date: June 14, 2009
My age: 47

Distance: 26.2 miles
Time: 3:52:00
Age-graded time: 3:33:24
Place: 43th
Finishers: 301

Notes: For a number of years, Fiddlehead and I went to the Phuket Marathon together. Even though I wasn't in great shape, I joined him to help keep his streak of consecutive races going. With the completion of this run, I finally reached my goal of averaging at least one marathon race per year for my entire life.

48. Rutledge Marathon:
    Rutledge, Tennessee

Date: November 14, 2009
My age: 48
Distance: 26.2 miles
Time: 3:18:28
Age-graded time: 3:00:58
Place: 4th
Finishers: 150

Notes: I drove to this race from Savannah. The course featured rolling hills in beautiful countryside. It was nice to get a top-five finish. I just missed the podium.

49. Tucson Marathon:
    Tucson, Arizona

Date: December 15, 2010
My age: 49
Distance: 26.2 miles
Time: 3:10:03
Age-graded time: 2:51:46
Place: 46th

Finishers: 1,246

Notes: I couldn't come close to equaling my time in my previous Tucson Marathon. The run still ranked as one of my top age-graded performances.

50. Boston Marathon:
    Hopkinton, Massachusetts

    Date: April 19, 2010
    My age: 49
    Distance: 26.2 miles
    Time: 3:15:36
    Age-graded time: 2:56:02
    Place: 3,692nd
    Finishers: 22,849

    Notes: I finally achieved my goal of running the Boston Marathon ten times. Would this be the last time that I heard Rocky Music, the Eye of the Tiger, and the Chariots of Fire theme song along the streets of Boston? The Boston Marathon means a lot to me. I was lucky to experience it ten times. It's more than just a race, having been run since 1897. And, with the tragedy that occurred in 2013, the importance and symbolic nature of the run has increased. It's a truly international marathon—one that all runners want to add to their palmarès.

51. Phuket Marathon:
    Phuket, Thailand

    Date: June 13, 2010
    My age: 49
    Distance: 26.2 miles
    Time: 3:54:11
    Age-graded time: 3:31:39
    Place: 55th

Finishers: 394

Notes: I accompanied Fiddlehead to yet another Phuket Marathon.

52. Baltimore Marathon:
    Baltimore, Maryland

    Date: October 15, 2011
    My age: 50
    Distance: 26.2 miles
    Time: 3:26:07
    Age-graded time: 3:03:54
    Place: 194th
    Runners: 5,000 (approximate)

    Notes: Although not training for a marathon, I was living in Annapolis, so decided to jump into the nearby race. Considering my lack of conditioning, I ran a decent time on the scenic course.

53. Khon Kaen Marathon:
    Khon Kaen, Thailand

    Date: January 29, 2012
    My age: 50
    Distance: 26.2 miles
    Time: 3:21:14
    Age-graded time: 2:59:32
    Place: 82nd
    Runners: 578

    Notes: Although no longer training for the marathon, I was cycling an incredible amount. I ran a good race in Khon Kaen. The top twenty or so finishers were from Kenya and Ethiopia. With me entering a new age group, I placed well. I was so strong that right after finishing, I drove to Phu Kradueng Mountain and made the arduous ascent and descent. Rangers told me it was too late to start up the mountain, as I arrived post-race in the afternoon. But, I assured the national-park staff that I'd make it up and down before dark.

While I was climbing, a number of groups coming down warned me about heading up so late. They were trying to be helpful. After I summited, I passed them on the descent. I didn't get caught in the dark, but they did. I never mentioned that I ran a marathon that morning.

As of this writing, this race is the last one where I broke three hours for my age-graded time. I'm confident it won't be my last time.

54. Sukhothai Marathon:
Sukhothai, Thailand

Date: June 26, 2016
My age: 54
Distance: 26.2 miles
Time: 3:41:00
Age-graded time: 3:10:18
Place: 17th
Age group: 2nd
Runners: 600 (approximate)

Notes: With my ongoing, intense focus on cycling, I hadn't run a marathon for almost four and a half years. This was the longest gap in my marathon-running career since I ran my first marathon on home soil in Rhode Island in 1989. My 24-year streak of running at least one marathon every year from 1989-2012 ended four years earlier. As I mentioned in the introductory remarks of this chapter, I achieved the streak without being aware of it.

I often said to myself that from the age of 28 onward, I could have run a marathon on any day. I believe that statement to be true. Thus if I'd been paying closer attention to my streak, I easily could have kept it alive. In fact, during the intervening years, when I didn't run a marathon race, I did run farther than the marathon distance in training. Most years I ran over the ultra-distance as well. I used this race as preparation for my upcoming Ironman.

When I completed my 54th marathon, I was 54 years old. One month after this race, my average number of marathons dropped below one per year. I hope to bring it back up to one marathon per year for the remainder of my life. After the COVID-19 pandemic is under control, I may start a new streak. My record of 24 years straight is probably out of reach. But, I may give it a go.

In Thailand in order to increase participation and maximize profits, it has become common to hold a marathon, half marathon, ten K, and five K concurrently on the same course. Since many of the "runners" in the five- and ten-K races are walkers, the roads get congested. The staggered start times are such that the fields overlap at the end. I weaved all over the road for the last ten kilometers to get through the pack.

Aid stations run out of supplies, and marathoners who've been running for hours are competing with five-K walkers to get a drink. Although a beautiful, flat course in a national historic park, the race isn't designed with marathoners in mind. I highly recommend it for walkers or those running in the shorter events. The atmosphere is festive.

55. Lampang Marathon:
Lampang, Thailand

Date: October 25, 2020
My age: 59
Distance: 26.2 miles
Time: 4:21:08
Age-graded time: 3:34:42
Place: 107th
Age group: 15/53
Runners: 387

Notes: I jumped into this marathon with Sanpawat "Bobby" Kantabutra, but I'd done *no* run training. I got Bobby into marathon running about ten years earlier. When he suggested it, I couldn't pass up the opportunity. I had just finished my longest ride to date—a solo, epic push of 4,500+ miles in Thailand—on a mountain bike. That ride left me strong as an ox. I knew I could run a marathon. I went out pretty hard, and of course, suffered from about 15 miles onward. After the run I was sore for five days. Bobby struggled with a leg injury, but hung in there for a gutsy finish.

In hindsight I'm really glad we did the run, as the COVID-19 pandemic has made it difficult to enter any athletic events. My age-graded time of 3:34:42 was slower than I ran my first marathon. However, with minimal run training, I could chop 30 minutes off my time. I'm in better shape at age 60 than I was in my late 20s.

8. Road/Shorter Trail Races

> "I think my legs fell off. If you see them back there, please move them to the side of the trail. Thanks."

I focused my running on ultra-marathons and marathons, but along the way I ran shorter races as speed work. While in high school, I ran cross-country. My best mile is a 4:38, and my best 10K a 34:31. My fastest half marathon is my split from the 2005 Tucson Marathon, where I went through in 1:18:00. As I get older, I'll focus more on shorter distances. In total I spent the equivalent of two full years hobbling around, struggling to go down stairs after endurance events. The beauty of shorter races is they're over quickly, and you don't develop debilitating soreness. They're easier. There are more options available. Entry fees are less too.

Note that for a few events in this chapter I estimated the number of finishers. In these cases I failed at tracking down exact values, and the information wasn't available to me at the race. This list isn't comprehensive. I don't have my results for events prior to 1992.

1. <u>New England Athletics Congress 10M Championships:</u> Newburyport, Massachusetts

Date: July 28, 1992
My age: 31
Distance: 10 miles
Time: 1:03:15
Place: 200th (approximate)
Finishers: 2,400 (approximate)

Notes: I never trained specifically for races shorter than a marathon so to average under 6:20 pace per mile was a good run. I enjoyed the fact that I wasn't sore for three or four days afterwards. I resumed training immediately.

2. Seven Sisters 12 Mile Trail Run:
   Amherst, Massachusetts

   Date: April 25, 1993
   My age: 31
   Distance: 12 miles
   Time: 2:23:54
   Place: 10th
   Finishers: 111

   Notes: This is a beautiful and difficult course, having a steeply uphill start. I went anaerobic after 30 seconds. I guess the 9th place runner was far ahead of me, as I got lost several times. That certainly didn't help me catch him. The course is an out-and-back with seven hills each way. The trail is rocky, and if you take risks on the downhills, there's a good chance of falling. For a while, Fish worked at Amherst College. My mother was born in North Hampton. I enjoyed going to this part of Massachusetts.

3. Seven Sisters 12 Mile Trail Run:
   Amherst, Massachusetts

   Date: May 1, 1994
   My age: 32
   Distance: 12 miles
   Time: 2:06:55
   Place: 5th
   Finishers: 135

Notes: After a good run here the year before, I came back with my friend Ellen Hepp and a few of her friends. The race director offered to wager a six pack of beer with anyone who thought they could break two hours. Wisely I didn't take him up. A sub-2:07 on this course is a good achievement. Ellen ran a good race. One of her friends became angry at me because the course is so difficult.

4. <u>New England Half Marathon Championships:</u>
   Newport, Rhode Island

   Date: September 30, 1996
   My age: 35
   Distance: 13.1 miles
   Time: 1:22:56
   Place: 78th
   Finishers: 700 (approximate)

   Notes: Back on home soil, this was a solid run. It works out to about 6:20 pace per mile.

5. <u>Market Square 10K:</u>
   Portsmouth, New Hampshire

   Date: June 14, 1997
   My age: 35
   Distance: 6.2 miles
   Time: 37:51
   Place: 54th
   Runners: 1,456

   Notes: I ran a 6:05 pace per mile.

6. <u>Derry 16 Miler:</u>
   Derry, New Hampshire

   Date: January 25, 1998

My age: 36
Distance: 16 miles
Time: 1:54:02
Place: 44th
Runners: 367

Notes: I spent Christmas in Italy. Right after returning home, my friend Patrick Messer and I jumped into this race. The temperatures were well-below freezing, and the roads were covered in black ice. Because the course is hilly, we slipped and slid every which way. We ran together. We laughed. At the finish Patrick beat me. When the results came out, I was listed ahead of him. We laughed about that too.

7. <u>Mount Washington Road Race:</u>
   Mount Washington, New Hampshire

Date: June 20, 1998
My age: 36
Distance: 7.6 miles
Time: 1:18:17
Place: 41st
Finishers: 721

Notes: Entries for this race are limited. I was lucky to get a number in the lottery. They say this is a race with only one hill. There's an elevation gain of 4,650 feet with an average gradient of 12%. The steepest section touches 18% and is called the Raymond Grade. I ran well and finished just behind Olympic-gold medalist and former marathon world-record holder Joan Benoit Samuelson. My goal was to avoid walking, and I achieved it. I was always a better uphill than downhill runner.

8. <u>Armstrong Atlantic State University Homecoming 5K:</u>
   Savannah, Georgia

Date: January 30, 1999
My age: 37
Distance: 3.1 miles
Time: 17:59
Place: 3rd
Finishers: 50 (approximate)

Notes: This time equates to a 5:48 pace per mile. I made the podium.

9. Shamrock 5K:
    Savannah, Georgia

    Date: March 12, 1999
    My age: 37
    Distance: 3.1 miles
    Time: 17:53
    Place: 15th
    Finishers: 175 (approximate)

    Notes: This time equates to a 5:46 pace per mile. It was a good performance, as Savannah is starting to get hot and humid by mid-March.

10. Savannah Bridge Run 10K:
    Savannah, Georgia

    Date: May 1, 1999
    My age: 37
    Distance: 6.2 miles
    Time: 39:04
    Place: 24th
    Finishers: 1,591

    Notes: This was a good time on a course with two big hills, going over the Savannah Bridge and returning. I finished in the top 1.5%.

11. Akranes Half Marathon:
Akranes, Iceland

Date: June 12, 1999
My age: 37
Distance: 13.1 miles
Time: 1:26:09
Place: 4th
Finishers: 100 (approximate)

Notes: During the summer of 1999, I lived in Reykjavik. I became involved with numerous running groups. My friend Olaf was from Akranes up in the north. We decided to run his hometown half marathon. It's a beautiful, scenic course. I finished in the top five and just missed the podium.

12. Armstrong Atlantic State University Homecoming 5K:
Savannah, Georgia

Date: February 19, 2000
My age: 38
Distance: 3.1 miles
Time: 18:38
Place: 6th
Finishers: 50 (approximate)

Notes: This time equates to a 6:01 pace per mile.

13. Savannah Bridge Run 10K:
Savannah, Georgia

Date: May 6, 2000
My age: 38
Distance: 6.2 miles
Time: 39:43

Place: 22nd
Finishers: 1,363

Notes: This was another good, hard bridge run in Savannah, where I finished in the top 1.6%.

14. <u>Tybee Half Marathon:</u>
Tybee Island, Georgia

Date: February 3, 2001
My age: 39
Distance: 13.1 miles
Time: 1:22:23
Place: 19th
Finishers: 645

Notes: Although I would run this split frequently in marathons, it was one of my fastest half marathons. I ran the first half of my full-marathon races at top speed.

15. <u>Armstrong Atlantic State University Homecoming 5K:</u>
Savannah, Georgia

Date: February 10, 2001
My age: 39
Distance: 3.1 miles
Time: 18:27
Place: 1st
Finishers: 40 (approximate)

Notes: I won a race. The time equates to a 5:58 pace per mile.

16. <u>Shamrock 5K:</u>
Savannah, Georgia

Date: March 9, 2001

My age: 39
Distance: 3.1 miles
Time: 18:04
Place: 12th
Finishers: 150 (approximate)

Notes: This time equates to a 5:50 pace per mile.

17. Azalea 10K:
    Savannah, Georgia

    Date: March 24, 2001
    My age: 39
    Distance: 6.2 miles
    Time: 37:46
    Place: 8th
    Finishers: 125 (approximate)

    Notes: This time equates to a 6:06 pace per mile.

18. Savannah Bridge Run 10K:
    Savannah, Georgia

    Date: May 5, 2001
    My age: 39
    Distance: 6.2 miles
    Time: 39:45
    Place: 29th
    Finishers: 993

    Notes: I ran another solid race at one of Savannah's most popular events.

19. Armstrong Atlantic State University Homecoming 5K:
    Savannah, Georgia

Date: January 26, 2002
My age: 40
Distance: 3.1 miles
Time: 18:46
Place: 2nd
Finishers: 40 (approximate)

Notes: I was running together with my friend Phillip Schretter, who's a world-class beach-volleyball player. After a mile and a half, he said: "Your shoe's untied." Phillip wasn't joking. I stopped to tie my shoe. That was the last time I saw him until the finish. Phillip assured me he wasn't trying to gain an advantage, but just trying to prevent me from tripping. We laughed. It was a rookie mistake on my part. I always double knot my shoes, but somehow, on this day the knots came undone. Phillip deserved the win, and he may have beaten me anyway.

20. Shamrock 5K:
    Savannah, Georgia

Date: March 8, 2002
My age: 40
Distance: 3.1 miles
Time: 18:46
Place: 11th
Finishers: 150 (approximate)

Notes: Amazingly, this time was identical to my time run from two months earlier. Given the warmer conditions though, this effort was better.

21. High Mountain Institute 25K/50K:
    Leadville, Colorado

Date: July 13, 2002
My age: 40

Distance: 25K
Time: 2:23:28
Place: 3rd (1st master)
Finishers: 75 (approximate)

Notes: This is a hilly and tough race run at high altitude. I ran well and won the Masters division. I made it onto the overall podium as well.

22. <u>Trick or Trot 10K:</u>
Savannah, Georgia

Date: November 1, 2002
My age: 41
Distance: 6.2 miles
Time: 37:40
Place: 2nd (1st master)
Finishers: 125 (approximate)

Notes: This time equates to a 6:01 pace per mile. I won the Masters division and took second-place overall. It felt good to finish on the podium again.

23. <u>Savannah Bridge Run 10K:</u>
Savannah, Georgia

Date: December 7, 2002
My age: 41
Distance: 6.2 miles
Time: 39:37
Place: 26th
Finishers: 581

Notes: I ran eight seconds faster than two years prior. It felt good to dip under 40 minutes after age 40.

24. Run for the Children 10K:
Savannah, Georgia

Date: September 21, 2003
My age: 42
Distance: 6.2 miles
Time: 41:10
Place: 6th (1st master)
Finishers: 150

Notes: This was a run for a good cause. The course was long. I won the Masters division.

25. Savannah Bridge Run 10K:
Savannah, Georgia

Date: December 6, 2003
My age: 42
Distance: 6.2 miles
Time: 38:36
Place: 17th (3rd Master)
Finishers: 650

Notes: This was an excellent time for my age and this course. I finished in the prize money and won $100 for my third-place Masters finish. It's the fastest of my five bridge runs in Savannah. I carried my fitness over from my PCT hike.

26. Azalea 10K:
Savannah, Georgia

Date: March 27, 2004
My age: 42
Distance: 6.2 miles
Time: 41:02
Place: 3rd

Finishers: 150 (approximate)

Notes: When I was leading and near the lead, I made two wrong turns. These mistakes may have cost me a place. They did cost me time. It was another beautiful run in Savannah in high heat and humidity. I believe that I won the Masters division. I finished on the podium.

27. Governor's Cup Half Marathon:
Columbia, South Carolina

Date: October 15, 2005
My age: 44
Distance: 13.1 miles
Time: 1:25:26
Place: 12th (1st in division, 2nd master)
Finishers: 800 (approximate)

Notes: On the morning of this race, I drove up to South Carolina. I wasn't familiar with the course. It ends with a steep hill, and the finish is around a corner. I should have won the Masters division, but I wasn't sure how much farther it was to the finish. I was passed near the end. I had plenty of fight left. When I saw the finish line, I realized that I should have pushed the last hill harder, but by then it was too late. My chance for a Masters division win eluded me.

28. Skidaway Institute of Oceanography 10K:
Skidaway Island, Georgia

Date: October 22, 2005
My age: 44
Distance: 6.2 miles
Time: 39:47
Place: 3rd (1st master)
Finishers: 100 (approximate)

Notes: Given the extreme heat and humidity, this was a solid run. The two runners who beat me were college runners. I couldn't have beaten them. I won the Masters division. It felt good to be on the podium with the collegians.

29. Eastern States 20 Miler:
    Kittery, Maine

    Date: March 29, 2009
    My age: 47
    Distance: 20 miles
    Time: 2:22:06
    Place: 55th
    Finishers: 573

    Notes: This event was added to New England's running calendar as a tune-up for the Boston Marathon. The race took place on a cold and rainy early spring day. I ran well. While waiting for Tarman's son Peter to finish, the cold-ocean breeze chilled me. I almost became hypothermic. I wrapped up in a garbage bag. I was shivering by the time we reconnected. This course follows the New Hampshire coastline and has wonderful scenery.

30. Annapolis 10 Miler:
    Annapolis, Maryland

    Date: August 29, 2010
    My age: 49
    Distance: 10 miles
    Time: 1:10:27
    Place: 175th
    Finishers: 4,581

    Notes: The entry fee is rather steep for this event. Each finisher is given a high-quality shirt. Of course, I have hundreds of shirts from races. Before my Dad passed away, I gave him my shirts. People often asked him if he competed. He proudly told them that his son was an Ironman, an ultra-marathoner, or a marathoner, depending on which shirt he was wearing.

I was involved in a sprint finish with a strong, young guy. He leaned and got me at the tape. We smiled. We shook hands and became friends. When I looked up the official results, I'd beaten him by a few seconds. The chip timing indicated that I started behind him. I often visited his candy store in downtown Annapolis, and we joked about the finish.

31. Doi Suthep 11K:
Chiang Mai, Thailand

Date: February 5, 2012
My age: 50
Distance: 11K
Time: 54:15
Place: 25th (approximate)
Finishers: 500 (approximate)

Notes: The Thai word 'Doi' means 'mountain.' This run ascends to the Doi Suthep temple. It's uphill the entire route, climbing a total of 2,238 feet. When I'm in Chiang Mai, I train on this mountain regularly. I knew the course. I just missed out on the prize money, which would have been 300 baht or about ten dollars. I was the second-place finisher over 50.

32. Phuket Mini-Marathon 11.4K:
Phuket, Thailand

Date: May 12, 2013
My age: 51
Distance: 11.4K
Time: 1:26
Place: 500 (approximate)

Finishers: 700 (approximate)

Notes: Kig had entered the five-kilometer race. I suggested that I pace her in the 11-kilometer one. Reluctantly, she agreed. The heavens opened up, and it poured. On the flooded course, we ran in mid-calf deep water. Many runners dropped out. Kig wanted to quit, but I kept her going. She did an inspirational run. Unfortunately, by the time we arrived, the race organizers had run out of finisher's medals. That was too bad, as this was her first race.

For five days following the run, Kig had trouble walking. After this race she set a goal of running a half marathon every year. She's one of many people whom I've gotten involved in running and in taking care of their health.

33. Phayao Lake 26K:
    Phayao, Thailand

Date: May 29, 2016
My age: 54
Distance: 26.1K
Time: 2:09:15
Age group (50-59): 7/101
Place: 73rd
Runners: 1,001

Notes: This race is one lap around Phayao Lake in a lovely mountain setting. One of the Thai Princesses was running, so the start was delayed. Shortly after the start, I passed her and her ten-bodyguard entourage. The course is flat. The race is hot and humid. I ran a steady pace.

34. TuphaLap Half Marathon:
    San Kamphaeng, Thailand

Date: July 24, 2016
My age: 54

Distance: 21.5K (13.33 miles)
Time: 1:42:46
Age group (50-59): 6th
Place: 25th (approximate)
Runners: 250 (approximate)

Notes: The course is an out-and-back with two long, steep climbs. I ran well and finished strongly. It was hot and humid. There were many top-notch runners at this challenging race. Kig ran with her son in the 5K, and they tied for the win. After the race we went to the San Kamphaeng hot springs to recover. I was glad to have inspired her son to race.

35. Udon Thani Half Marathon:
    Udon Thani, Thailand

Date: May 7, 2017
My age: 55
Distance: 21.1K (13.1 miles)
Time: 1:43:30
Place: 42nd
Runners: 420

Notes: I cycled 700 miles in the week leading up to this race, including a 100-mile ride the day before. In hot and humid conditions, I ran hard with little run training. Although my legs were fatigued from my recent cycling, I felt strong the entire race. This was an outstanding effort and under the conditions a respectable time. If my legs were rested, I'm sure that I was in 1:35 shape. This equates to an age-graded time of 1:20:26 and ranks right up there with my best half marathons ever. This run was part of my buildup for the Swissman Extreme Triathlon, which is considered the world's hardest Ironman-distance triathlon. I entered that race in outstanding shape.

36. Run for Heart Nakornping Hospital Mini-Marathon 12K:

Chiang Mai, Thailand

Date: September 17, 2017
My age: 56
Distance: 12.8K (7.94 miles)
Time: 1:17:00
Place: 400th (approximate, pacing Kig)
Finishers: 2,500 (approximate)

Notes: The roughly eight-mile distance is a strange one. Conditions were hot and humid. I paced Kig, and she ran well. I wasn't used to running so far back in the pack. It was a nice training run for me.

37. Follow King Number 9 9.9K:
Udon Thani, Thailand

Date: October 8, 2017
My age: 56
Distance: 9.9K
Time: 57:15
Place: 300th (approximate, pacing Kig)
Finishers: 3,500 (approximate)

Notes: The long-serving Thai king Rama IX was extremely ill. Many Thais, including non-runners, came out to show their love for him. It was an emotional start and finish. I paced Kig to what would have been her PR in the 10K, a sub-58. However, the course was 100 meters short. Conditions were hot and humid.

38. Lanna Half Marathon:
Chiang Mai, Thailand

Date: November 19, 2017
My age: 56
Distance: 21.1K

Time: 2:11:12
Place: 150th (an estimate, pacing Kig)
Finishers: 750 (approximate)

Notes: I paced and muled for Kig. She started fast. I grabbed drinks. She stayed well hydrated. Kig ran strongly through 17K. At that point with me blocking the view, she stopped for a bathroom break. She insisted on walking, but I insisted on running. Kig ran and showed a lot of courage. I got tough on her. She held it together. I knew she could run all the way to the finish. Kig set a PR and was proud of her performance. I was proud of her, too. She thanked me.

39. Chiang Mai Half Marathon:
    Chiang Mai, Thailand

Date: December 25, 2017
My age: 56
Distance: 21.1K
Time: 1:43:12
Place: 69th
Finishers: 1,978

Notes: I started fast around the city's 700-year-old moat. I wanted to dip under 1:40. I was well ahead of my goal pace for the first 12K. After that due to my fast start, the heat, and the humidity, I faded. In the closing stages of the race, I got passed a number of times, which is unusual. There was nothing that I could do except shake my head. I finished in the top 4%.

Kig ran the 10K race with her son Jamie. She paced him. In the last kilometer, he wanted to quit. She told him that the faster he ran, the sooner his suffering would end. He outkicked her to break one hour. Kig followed closely behind.

40. Asia Justice Half Marathon:
    Chiang Mai, Thailand

Date: December 9, 2018
My age: 57
Distance: 21.1K
Time: 1:47:14
Place: 10th
Finishers: 200 (approximate)

Notes: This run is for a good cause. Although December, it was another warm and humid day in Thailand. I often train on parts of this course. Toward the end there's an out-and-back section along a dirt road. Unfortunately, it was paved over in 2020. The area is becoming commercialized. The road goes uphill to an entrance of Doi Suthep-Doi Pui National Park. I pushed hard on that uphill section and passed a couple of runners. I finished strongly to make it into the top ten.

    Kig ran too. I didn't pace her until the end. After my finish I ran back a couple miles to meet her. From there I paced her to the finish. She ran well. I ended up getting in a nice four-mile cooldown. Kig talked about how brutal the climb had been to the park's entrance. I told her that was where I'd made my move in the race. We laughed.

9. Multi-Sport and Triathlon

"Does anyone have a spare pair of goggles?"

I always loved to run and ride a bicycle. When I was 14 years old, I joined a swim team. My passion for swimming developed under Fish's influence, but I was slower to take to the water than to land-based sports. When I learned about triathlon in the 1980s, I immediately became interested. As a young boy, I often rode my bicycle to our Swim & Tennis Club, swam, played tennis and basketball, went for a run, and then cycled home.

Combining three sports came naturally to me. Although I thought I was a better runner than swimmer or cyclist, in the triathlon world, I fared better in the swim. When I took up cycling seriously, my running suffered. I was still competitive in the swim though. After completing a swim workout, I always feel invigorated. The workouts are easier on my joints and help increase flexibility. When training at an indoor pool, the weather isn't a factor. At my job it was usually easy to sneak in a swim at lunchtime. Over time, I began swimming more than Fish.

I focused on endurance races. I never competed in a triathlon as short as the Olympic distance—1.5K swim, 40K bike, and 10K run. My first triathlon was a half Ironman, and from there I immediately graduated to the Ironman distance—2.4-mile swim, 112-mile bike, and a 26.2-mile run. Note that because the Ironman was developed in the US, its distances are expressed in imperial units.

After completing a number of Ironman-distance events, I set a goal of a sub-10 hour performance. My best swim time in the Ironman is a 54:14; my best bike split is a 5:18:02; my best run is a 3:52:36. Combining all three and adding five minutes for transitions gives me a theoretical Ironman time of 10:09:52. I still need to find ten minutes.

In addition to problems such as crashing during the bike segment, a broken zipper on my wetsuit, broken goggles, a loose headset on my bike, aid stations running out of supplies, and getting lost on the run, I always entered Ironman races with hot and humid conditions and/or ones with hilly or mountainous courses. The weather and course undulations were simply the nature of the Ironman races that I was able to enter. The Ironman wasn't designed to be easy; it was designed to be hard. The founders pit endurance athletes from three different disciplines against one another to find out which sport—swimming, cycling, or running—had the better-conditioned athletes.

In the early days of triathlon, of course, few races existed. It was and still is difficult to gain entry. One needs to enter a race a year in advance. And, on the day of signup, one must be ready at the keyboard, as soon as registration opens. Due to bad timing, I missed out on several occasions. It was frustrating being fit to race yet being unable to secure an entry for one of the limited slots. The demand far exceeds the available positions, especially for the more popular events, which explains why the entry fees are so high ($700) compared to other sports.

There are fast courses that I never got a chance to race. For example, the Roth Challenge in Germany and Ironman Western Australia are races that I would have liked to have done. After I set the goal of a sub-10 hour Ironman, I pushed myself harder in training than I would have otherwise. My goal left me striving to improve. In 2021 I got into perhaps the best triathlon shape of my life, as I prepared for Ironman Estonia. I selected this race due to its cooler weather. Despite my age, I felt optimistic.

I trained hard for ten months for Ironman Estonia. I worked on my time-trial position on the bike. I met with a coach. I dieted. I put in huge training weeks. Unfortunately, I wasn't able to get vaccinated for the coronavirus in Thailand, where I was training. At the age of 60, I knew it unlikely that I could ever achieve this level of fitness again. And, while entering a new age group, I dreamed of qualifying for the World Championships. Although in the best shape of my life, I couldn't race. I felt terribly disappointed to have to withdraw from Ironman Estonia.

After my last few Ironman-distance triathlons, I said after each one it would be my last race. I've been competing in triathlon in five decades. After my incredible preparation and disappointment with Ironman Estonia, now I'm not sure. It's difficult to get motivated to train hard enough to compete. It's not in my nature to enter a race with the goal of finishing. I like to perform my best. The Ironman requires a big time commitment. The pandemic and time will tell. I'll keep training.

Next I provide my best splits for half-Ironman and full-Ironman distance races.

- Best splits in the half Ironman:
  - Swim: 25:00
  - Bike: 2:43:36
  - Run: 1:23:41

- Best splits in the Ironman:
  - Swim: 54:14
  - Bike: 5:18:02
  - Run: 3:52:36

Note that in the Ironman my bike spilt of 5:18:02 divided in half is 2:39:01. This is faster than I ever went in the half Ironman. In fact I once went through the half-Ironman distance on the bike in the full Ironman in 2:30:00. I never held back on the bike. Following are my best finishes in multi-sport and triathlon events:

- 5th place Wildman Biathlon, 1997
- 14th overall Tupper Lake Tinman (half-Ironman distance), 1997
- 5th place Espirit Triathlon (Ironman distance), 2001
- 1st place age-group Chesapeake Man Endurance Festival (now Ironman Maryland), 2011
- 1st place swim age-group Ironman Taiwan, 2016
- 1st place bike age-group Ironman Taiwan, 2016

- 5th place overall age-group Ironman Taiwan, 2016
- 1st place age-group Swissman Extreme (Ironman distance), 2017
- 1st place age-group swim, Laguna Phuket Triathlon, 2020
- 1st place age-group bike, Laguna Phuket Triathlon, 2020
- 1st place age-group overall, Laguna Phuket Triathlon, 2020

Next I provide a listing of my multi-sport and triathlon competitions with the usual accompanying information.

1. Black Hills Triathlon:
    Olympia, Washington

    Date: August 1988
    My age: 27
    Distances: 1-mile swim, 58-mile bike, 13.1-mile run
    Time: 4:51:00
    Swim split: 25:00
    Bike split: 2:55:00
    Run split: 1:30
    Place: 40th
    Finishers: 220 (approximate)

    Notes: This is one of the world's oldest triathlons. The weekend before the race, I went out and completed the entire course. I swam alone in the lake, hammered the bike route, and had Claire pace me for the run. The effort took something out of me. I was glad to preview the course though, so I knew what to expect.

    As I mentioned in the mountaineering chapter, when I was 14 years old, I began wearing glasses. My vision was poor: 20/800. For open-water swimming, I needed prescription goggles to see well enough to stay on course. I left my glasses at the exit of the swim. I wore my goggles until I reached the volunteers. In the process of retrieving my glasses, I always lost time in transition. The prescriptions in my swim goggles and glasses weren't identical.

When I started the bike segment, this difference resulted in blurry vision.

The run course is hilly, and this was my first half-Ironman race. The training weekend was the first time that I'd completed a triathlon at the half-Ironman distance. This was my first triathlon competition. I raced on my road bike and understood nothing about aerodynamics. Despite my residual fatigue from the course preview, I performed well. My energy remained high. Once my legs loosened up, I ran well. Although still a novice, I fell in love with triathlon. I could see that I had a lot to learn.

As of this writing, I've only raced in two other half-Ironman races. However, I've gone the half-Ironman distance about 50 times in training. I've completed the swim and bike segments of the Ironman dozens of times in training, but never with the full run. On such days I usually only run two or three miles. Although fit to race on many occasions, the logistics, cost, and limited availability of triathlon slots meant I couldn't take advantage of my fitness.

2. Bay State Triathlon:
   Medford, Massachusetts

Date: August 13, 1990
My age: 29
Distances: 1.2-mile swim, 42-mile bike, 10-mile run
Time: 3:30:09
Swim split: 27:48
Bike split: 1:53:14
Run split: 1:08:27
Age group: 22nd
Finishers: 118 (in age group)

Notes: I raced against The Terminator. When he lapped me near the end of his second and final loop on the run, I stayed with him for about 100 yards. I was running 6:45 per mile pace, but he was running 5:30 per mile, as he kicked in for the win. I had five miles to run still. Although I paid for my short burst, it was fun to run with one of the legends of the sport, if only for 100 yards.

3. Ironman Canada:
    Penticton, British Columbia, Canada

    Date: August 26, 1990
    My age: 29
    Distances: 2.4-mile swim, 112-mile bike, 26.2-mile run
    Time: 11:05:01
    Swim split: 58:32
    Bike split: 6:03:13 (both transitions)
    Run split: 4:03:16
    Place: 209th
    Finishers: 854

    Notes: I'd entered the 1989 race, but due to a patella-tendon injury, I withdrew. That's right, I planned to race in the Ironman before I'd even run a marathon. My knee bothered me on the bike, where the injury first manifested itself from riding too big a gear. During the fall of 1989, I was able to recover enough to run my first marathon. When I took on the Ironman, I had one road marathon under my belt. I was one of the least experienced competitors.

    In Penticton I raced against some Ironman legends, including ST and Erin Baker. I performed well in the swim and exited the water in a good place. At mile 10 I crashed on a set of railroad tracks. I hadn't known the route crossed tracks. I damaged both wheels, and I lost my water bottles. I suffered road rash and bruises. I released my rim brakes, so they wouldn't rub as much. I straightened my handlebars. I dusted myself off. I got back on. I kept riding. I shook my head and thought: "Only 100 miles to go."

    While descending Richter Pass, my wheels shimmied terribly. One competitor yelled: "You pussy," because I descended so cautiously. Although I wanted to give him the finger, I ignored him. I had no choice if I wanted to maintain control of my bicycle. I dared not look up or take a hand off my handlebars. I got the dry heaves on that descent. Each time I went to puke, my eyes closed involuntarily. On a sinuous descent with damaged wheels, it wasn't a good situation. Several times I lost control and almost crashed.

I felt relieved to start the run. Even though I hadn't been able to take on fuel during the bike segment, I ran a solid marathon. It was just my second marathon. It probably helped that I couldn't push the bike ride as hard as I'd intended. Of course, the crash affected my gait. I wasn't going to drop out of my first Ironman though. Once running, I was able to take on fluids. I ran just 40 minutes slower than in my first marathon. I easily would have broken 11 hours, if I hadn't crashed.

The Ironman wasn't well-known in 1990. I felt like a champion for having finished. The Wide World of Sports TV show had built up the Ironman as one of the hardest endurance tests in the world. I believed them. No one in my circles had ever heard of it. I overcame adversity to complete the Ironman on a mountainous course in hot, sunny conditions. I kept my achievement to myself. From that moment on though, I was an Ironman. I'd done what many consider impossible. I'm an Ironman.

It meant a lot to finish Ironman Canada. I trained alone and received no coaching. It was a fresh experience. Back then, there was little information available about triathlon. There weren't any popular magazines, and of course, the World Wide Web didn't exist. Now there's an abundance of information freely available, about how to train and get mentally ready for the Ironman. Like most other triathletes at the time, I did it on my own. I didn't even know any triathletes. Completing this race was a defining moment in my life and athletic career.

4. Endurance Triathlon:
Sunapee, New Hampshire

Date: September 9, 1991
My age: 30
Distances: 2.4-mile swim, 112-mile bike, 26.2-mile run
Time: 11:19:12

Swim split: 54:14 (8th out of the water)
Bike split: 6:02:37
Run split: 4:16:52
Place: 33rd
Finishers: 188 (approximate)

Notes: Fish and I entered this race together. His father Dapper Dan was there to support us. I was close to Fish's father. He watched me grow up. He cooked for us. Dapper teased us about dating. He chauffeured us around. We spent a lot of time horsing around together. He was a character. With Dapper on the sidelines cheering, I wanted to perform well.

Fish exited the water in 48 minutes—a time many top pros only dream of achieving—in first place. When I came out in eighth place, Dapper was shocked. I exited the water much sooner than he anticipated. He gave me a big smile and yelled: "Go, Greenie!" At around mile 80, I passed Fish on the bike. I handed him Advil for his lower-back pain. We chatted. We compared notes about aches and pains. We laughed and pedaled. After wishing each other good luck, I forged ahead.

The bicycle course was five loops around Lake Sunapee on an extremely hilly circuit. Back then, there was no GPS. According to my research, one loop has 1,532 feet of climbing and the maximum gradient is 9.5%. The race had about 8,000 feet of climbing in the form of sharp, steep hills. Due to stop signs, traffic, and 90° turns, many of the climbs were tackled without the advantage of a good-rolling start. On the last loop, I was out of the saddle grinding away.

Fish overtook me toward the end of the bike course. He rode well. After the climb to the bike to run transition, I sat down next to my bike. I could see I was near the top ten, as there were few bikes in the racks. I gathered myself and ate pretzels for the salt. Once regrouped, I took my favorite water bottle (the one from my first Western States 100) and ran back down the hill from the ski resort.

Within a few hundred yards, my upper body felt so trashed that I threw away the water bottle. I shook my head. The swim and bike course had fatigued my arms and shoulders to the point where I couldn't carry anything. I could barely swing my arms. My core felt weak. I badly misjudged my abilities. It wasn't the first time. After the race I hoped to go back and find the bottle. I never did.

I ran well, and I soon passed Fish. I held my own in the top ten. Due to work commitments, I'd missed the pre-race meeting. The run course consisted of small and big loops. When I came around the small loop for the third time, the race official said: "Wait a minute, you did three laps. You only needed to do two." WTF. I learned that I'd run an extra 2.5 miles. I asked why he didn't let me know on the previous lap, to prevent my mistake. He replied: "I didn't notice." I thanked him. I clinched my fists. I shook my head. It could have been worse; I might have done four loops.

I was furious with myself. Instead of running a marathon, I would be running 29 miles. Having finished the Western States 100 just three months earlier, I knew I was capable. I eventually passed Fish again. We provided each other encouragement. I didn't have time to explain my ordeal. He wondered how he'd gotten in front of me. I ran incredibly well despite the extra distance. I easily would have broken 11 hours, if not for my error. I may have finished in the top ten. This was one of my strongest days in triathlon. It was a day where I was near a lifetime peak in terms of strength—both mentally and physically.

At the finish a guy who I'd caught up to outsprinted me. He smiled. He felt happy to beat me. If not for my error, I would have beaten him by over 20 minutes. I congratulated him. I didn't go into the details about my extra loop. He enjoyed the moment. I felt strong. After my gross mistake, it would have been easy to crack or give up. I didn't. Once I got over the initial frustration, I adjusted well to my situation. I told myself to keep working away at it. I did that. This was my best run in the Ironman. On a flatter course and without my mistake, I might have dipped under 3:40 for the marathon.

Following right behind me, Fish arrived exhausted. He completed an inspirational race. We hobbled to dinner. While waiting in line, Fish spoke to the maître d': "I need something to eat. Right now. You can either give me some bread or drag my body out of here." A waiter arrived with bread, and we made it to our seats successfully. We laugh about that incident now. Back then, we were too busy eating to laugh.

5. Ironman Canada:
    Penticton, British Columbia, Canada

    Date: August 28, 1994
    My age: 33
    Distances: 2.4-mile swim, 112-mile bike, 26.2-mile run
    Time: 10:33:42
    Swim split: 59:41
    Bike split: 5:41:25 (both transitions)
    Run split: 3:52:36
    Place: 173th
    Finishers: 1,200 (approximate)

    Notes: Again I had the chance to compete against some of the top professionals in the sport. After my 54-minute, 8th place swim in my previous Ironman, I confidently started on the front row. While the national anthem played, the 1,000 competitors behind me pushed forward, and I ended up in chest-deep water. When the gun sounded, with a wall of bodies behind me, all I could do was flop forward. A few competitors swam over me, causing severe panic throughout my being. I held my breath. I waited. I hoped for an opening.

    After resurfacing and gulping in air, I sprinted for the next half mile. It wasn't until then that my heart rate slowed to a reasonable level. I burned a lot of unnecessary energy. I was happy to be alive. I felt relieved to be on my bike. Of course, I worried about the railroad tracks, where I'd crashed previously on this course. I bunny hopped and made it over them safely. I flew down Richter Pass, leaning into the corners and passing other riders. I had a solid bike ride.

During the run, I met an Australian competitor. Australia is known for its exceptional Ironman athletes. We ran together on the hot and sunny course. We chatted. I struggled with his accent. It took my mind off the suffering. I learned that he was an experienced Ironman. Eventually, I couldn't stay with him. He powered up a steep hill and left me behind. While grabbing plenty of fluids at the aid stations, I continued at a steady pace.

I set my PR of 10:33 in the Ironman that day. The bike course in Penticton involves the climb up Richter Pass. In August the course is hot and sunny. I believed if I could find a faster course, on a good day I could break ten hours. As I noted in the introductory remarks of this chapter, I set that as my goal. I wanted to go under ten hours, and I would give it my best shot. I kept training and dreaming.

6. Tupper Lake Tinman Triathlon:
Tupper Lake, New York

Date: July 19, 1997
My age: 35
Distances: 1.2-mile swim, 56-mile bike, 13.1-mile run
Time: 4:45:05
Swim split: 31:23
Bike split: 2:50:01 (both transitions)
Run split: 1:23:41
Place: 14th
Finishers: 141

Notes: At the start the conditions were akin to a London fog. It was easy to get lost in the lake. In modern times I doubt the officials would have permitted the race to start. The liability would be far too high. While being guided by voices of support staff in kayaks, I peered over waves through the mist trying to locate buoys. I heard a bell. It reminded me of a cowbell on a misty mountainside in Switzerland. I was relieved to exit the water.

Although the rolling hills tested me on the bike, I felt strong. The trisuit hadn't been invented yet, and I always spent about five minutes in each transition. I had a great run and was passing runners right up until the end. With each stride my legs loosened up. I felt like I was gliding. If the race had been a mile longer, I probably would have finished in the top 10.

Tarman raced with me. In fact he had a tight connection on a flight out of Boston immediately after the race. After I finished I loaded our bicycles and gear into his truck. When Tarman crossed the line, he jumped into the awaiting vehicle. I dropped him off on I-95, where Ironwoman intercepted us. She offered us her congratulations. She shook her head. We smiled.

I learned that Tarman made his flight to Paris. Although one of the few times when I won an award at a triathlon, we didn't have time to wait around for the ceremony. I never received my trophy. When Tarman disembarked at Charles de Gaulle, he could barely walk. I fared much better, as I only had a one-hour drive to drop off his truck in Maine. We later joked about the swim. I said: "Could you see anything?" Tarman said: "No, could you?" I said: "No, nothing. I went by Braille." He said: "Glad we survived." I agreed. We shook our heads.

7. Wildman Biathlon:
    Shelburne, New Hampshire

    Date: August 9, 1997
    My age: 36
    Distances: 6.2-mile run, 22.3-mile bike, 3-mile run
    Time: 2:32:00
    Run split: 39:00
    Bike split: 1:11:00
    Run split: 42:00
    Place: 5th
    Finishers: 67

Notes: The second run in this race is on a trail up the steep ski-slope of Wildcat Mountain. About a week before the race, I did a trial run of the course and that may have been a mistake. I wasn't recovered fully by race date. My parents drove up to New Hampshire from Rhode Island to watch me race. They took the gondola up Wildcat Mountain.

I pushed hard, as I wanted to perform well in front of my folks. At the finish Mom was on the verge of tears, seeing me nauseous from my effort. The elevation of Wildcat is 4,422 feet. We enjoyed good views. Tarman and Patrick raced with me. They finished strongly. We backslapped and shared a round robin of praises in the form of good job. The gondola ride down offered spectacular scenery and a welcome rest.

8. New England Triathlon Festival:
    Sunapee, New Hampshire

Date: August 23, 1997
My age: 36
Distances: 1-mile swim, 44-mile bike, 9-mile run
Time: 3:30:05
Swim split: 23:30
Bike split: 2:07:41 (both transitions)
Run split: 58:55
Place: 80th
Finishers: 552

Notes: I only competed in a few triathlons shorter than the half-Ironman distance. With fond memories of the Ironman-distance race at Sunapee, other than the extra loop on the run course, I decided to enter this event. I rode well on the hilly bike course. I averaged 6:30 pace per mile in the run, whereas in Ironman-distance races, I was running nine minutes per mile. In the Ironman I would stop to grab replenishment and walk a bit at aid stations, while refueling. Overall leg fatigue slowed my running speed down tremendously in the Ironman.

9. Greater Floridian Triathlon:
    Clermont, Florida

Date: October 24, 1998
My age: 37
Distances: 2.4-mile swim, 112-mile bike, 26.2-mile run
Time: 11:10:49
Swim split: 1:03:31
Transition one: 5:11
Bike split: 5:42:36
Transition two: 4:58
Run split: 4:14:36
Place: 95th
Finishers: 915

Notes: The middle of Florida is hilly. It's hot and humid. As I arrived at the front of the swim area for the start and began singing the national anthem, my prescription goggles broke in half. I couldn't fix them. With blurry vision I raced back to shore to the announcer. I asked him to announce that a competitor needed goggles. Within 30 seconds, five people who were there supporting athletes arrived and offered goggles.

I squinted and accepted a pair. I thanked the donor. While adjusting my gifted goggles, I hastily made my way through the wall of swimmers, all the way back to the front line. Without my prescription goggles, I wouldn't be able to see well. Before I had a chance to put my face in the water, the starter fired his gun.

With 1,000 swimmers behind me, I needed to sprint. When I put my face in the Floridian lake for the first time, I couldn't see anything. Nothing! The water is jet black from tannic acid leaching organic matter. Without vision correction things were even worse. My heart raced wildly. I stroked fast. I kicked hard.

Each time I put my face in the water, it was like putting my head into a black abyss. Squinting didn't help. With hundreds of swimmers thrashing around me, I teetered on panic. My personal reassurances weren't working. I said: "You'll be fine." But, I didn't believe it. I said: "Relax. Take is easy. Breathe." But, I couldn't.

When my face was in the water, I found myself closing my eyes. With my eyes shut, it wasn't any darker. I felt more comfortable. I concentrated on my stroke. I slowed my furious kick. While turning my head to breathe, I opened my eyes. I could see land. That helped. I could see sky. I avoided a panic attack and drowning.

After ten minutes of hard swimming, I moved ahead of most of the field. I found open water and was able to get my heartrate back under 200 beats per minute. The water hadn't changed, but I now knew it's black. The unfortunate incident of my broken goggles canceled my warm-up. I wasn't able to see well though, and I followed other swimmers rather than my own line. Amazingly the goggles didn't leak a drop.

When I exited the water, a volunteer handed me my glasses. Without them, I couldn't read the numbers on the bike racks. This was one reason I didn't leave my glasses at my bicycle. I needed to see in order to run to and collect my gear bag and find my bicycle. In big races fans weren't allowed near the transition area, so I had to leave my glasses with a volunteer. In the high temps of Central Florida, I rode well. I put in a solid run. After the race I looked for the person who had loaned me the goggles, but I couldn't find her.

Years later, after my Lasik surgery, I ended up using the gifted brand of goggles. In terms of comfort, they're much better than what I'd been using. As of this writing, I need eye correction again. My left eye can only be *corrected* to 20/100. I'm able to see well enough not to rely on prescription goggles. I see well enough out of my right eye that I can leave my glasses waiting for me in my bicycle helmet. This saves time.

Ever since this race, I bring multiple pairs of goggles to the swim. If I don't need them, one of my less-experienced competitors might. I'm more than happy to give away a pair of googles to pay it forward. Knowing that I have backup reduces my stress.

10. Greater Floridian Triathlon:
Clermont, Florida

Date: October 23, 1999
My age: 38
Distances: 2.4-mile swim, 112-mile bike, 26.2-mile run
Time: 11:37:37
Swim split: 1:07:07
Transition: 8:02
Bike split: 6:22:41
Transition: 4:24
Run split: 3:55:24
Place: 74th
Finishers: 600

Notes: I came back to race in Central Florida for the second time. I prepared for the opaque water by warming up. The swim was un-eventful. I experienced hot spots on my feet, which forced me to slow down on the bike. They were caused by a combination of stomping on the pedals too hard and the extreme heat, which caused my feet to swell. I stopped to massage my feet. This helped ease my pain. The massage stops resulted in a faster marathon. Tarman raced too. He recorded a solid finishing time.

11. Sea-to-Summit Triathlon:
    New Castle Island to Mount Washington, New Hampshire

Date: July 29, 2000
My age: 39
Distances: 12-mile kayak, 90-mile bike, 8.5-mile run
Time: 9:27:51
Kayak split: 2:00:58
Bike split (includes both transitions): 5:00:00
Run split: 2:26:53
Place: 11th
Entrants: 33

Notes: This race was by invitation only, and it had a select field of top athletes. The roads were open to traffic. The race finished on the summit of Mount Washington. I'd never done any serious kayaking before, so in preparation I took a lesson from a Navy SEAL. I told him to put me through the ringer, and he sure did. By the end of the lesson, I was Eskimo rolling and riding waves onto a beach. After my brutal working over by the Navy SEAL, my arms and shoulders were sore for days. Hooyah!

During the kayak segment of the race, I paddled well. I was in a borrowed touring kayak. I chose a good line through the wide open Great Bay. One needed to be careful of shallow water and getting stuck, due to the tides. The Piscataqua River is known for some of the strongest currents on the East Coast. Those with racing kayaks gained an advantage. I expended a lot of energy trying to keep pace.

When I mounted my bicycle, my hands were numb. My shoulders and arms ached. I stretched my back. I tried to brake. I couldn't. I shook out my hands. After a while, I regained feeling. Because the roads weren't closed to traffic, having braking ability was critical. I rode well on the hilly course. Ironwoman provided support, including handing me a much needed ham sandwich during the bike segment.

Tarman raced with me. His son Peter was to be my pacer up Mount Washington. As a safety measure, you're allowed to have someone run with you for the climb. I was moving too fast for a teenage Peter. I told him to meet me at the top. He arrived at the finish line about ten minutes after me and was in good spirits. The other racers on the course kept a watchful eye on him. While being paced by his daughter Jenny, Tarman finished well.

12. Esprit Triathlon:
    Montreal, Canada

Date: September 8, 2001
My age: 40
Distances: 2.4-mile swim, 112-mile bike, 26.2-mile run

Time: 10:53:25
Swim split: 1:03:23
Bike split: 5:18:02
Run split: 4:25:34
Place: 6th
Finishers: 55

Notes: Although it poured rain and we experienced major thunderstorms, I put in my fastest bike split in an Ironman-distance race. Due to the slick track, there were many crashes. I almost went down a number of times. I avoided numerous incidents, where riders fell directly in front of me. The day broke the record for the highest temperature ever recorded in Montreal. The heat index rocketed to over 135°F. The humidity was 100%, with steam rising off the pavement throughout the race.

My Mom and brother were there to support me. They searched out shade. On a ridiculously hot day, the good swim and fast bike allowed me to break 11 hours. Due to the weather conditions and bike crashes, many racers dropped out. This event was the only time that I finished in the top ten in an Ironman-distance race. I may have won my age group. We celebrated with a memorable steak dinner at one of the best restaurants in Montreal.

13. Ironman Arizona:
    Tempe, Arizona

Date: November 23, 2008
My age: 47
Distances: 2.4-mile swim, 112-mile bike, 26.2-mile run
Time: DNF
Swim split: 1:11:29
Bike split: 5:41:35
Run split: DNF, dropped out at mile 18

Notes: Although I hadn't raced in the Ironman for a number of years, I trained hard and was extremely fit. I planned to try and break ten hours. Due to crowded conditions, my race began with my worst swim ever in an Ironman. We swam in a narrow canal. After exiting the water, when I saw the race clock, it read 1:21. Although I tried to suppress negative self-talk, I couldn't. I said: "You did an outrageously slow swim." After the race I realized the clock that I'd seen was the time for the pros who had started ten minutes earlier than me. Although my swim was slower than normal, given the conditions, it wasn't actually terrible.

After my mediocre swim, I was behind schedule. In the desert in an effort to make up time, I pushed the bike segment hard and became badly dehydrated. I remember going up a hill at about eight miles per hour thinking: "This isn't acceptable." When I reached the turnaround, I traveled 35 mph downhill without pedaling. I'd been riding into a strong headwind. It was hard to overcome my negative emotions and self-talk. I continued to push the bike. While going full gas, I didn't refuel as much as I should have.

Before dismounting the bike, I programmed myself to run the entire marathon. I wouldn't walk a single step. In fact I didn't until I fell down at mile 13 with legs cramps. Covered in my own salt, I found myself in a difficult predicament. For a few miles, while trying to recover, I ate salt off my face. It didn't work. At the aid stations, I ate potato chips and pretzels and drank a salty broth, but it was too late. While feeling horrendous, I walked five more miles. My dream of breaking ten hours vanished. During the walk, I thought of surviving. My muscles seized up with cramps.

I believed that I could walk the last eight miles of the run, but I questioned the value/sanity of doing that. I came to the race to try to break ten hours. With badly cramped legs, it would take me at least two more hours to finish. I had seven hours until the cutoff. I considered my safety. I was badly dehydrated in the low humidity of the desert. I decided to drop out at mile 18.

Tarman finished. Ironwoman was there supporting us. After I dropped out, I ended up walking a few miles: to find her, to find Tarman, to collect gear, and to reach the hotel. I struggled to eat a slice of pizza. I was nauseous and had the chills, which reinforced I made the right decision. I did more than empty the tank. In hindsight, quitting was a good decision. I felt sick for days. As was often the case, I learned more in defeat than in victory.

14. Pumpkin Man Triathlon:
South Berwick, Maine

Date: September 12, 2010
My age: 49
Distances: 1.2-mile swim, 56-mile bike, 13.1-mile run
Time: 5:06:39
Swim split: 31:31
Hill climb run: 1:29
Transition one: 4:31
Bike split: 2:43:36
Transition two: 2:06
Run split: 1:44:54
Place: 84th
Finishers: 349

Notes: I jumped into this race on the spur of the moment to compete with Tarman and Patrick. Everyone had a successful race. We enjoyed a nice reunion. Tarman and Patrick's families cheered and celebrated with us at the finish. It felt good to return to New England to see my friends.

15. Ironman Louisville:
Louisville, Kentucky

Date: August 28, 2011
My age: 50
Distances: 2.4-mile swim, 112-mile bike, 26.2-mile run
Time: 12:21:24
Swim split: 1:05:30
Bike split: 5:44:36
Run split: 5:14:12
Place: 755th

Competitors: 2,437

Notes: This race drew a huge field. I had a fair swim and an okay bike. I fell apart on the run. The high heat and humidity affected me. I overcooked things on the hilly bike course. During the run, I learned that someone had died during the swim. That left a funny feeling inside. Tarman crewed for me and helped get me to the finish. Due to the tough conditions, many competitors dropped out. I hadn't set any time goals and never considered dropping out. After the race we enjoyed Louisville.

16. Chesapeake Man Endurance Festival:
Cambridge, Maryland

Date: September 24, 2011
My age: 50
Distances: 2.4-mile swim, 112-mile bike, 26.2-mile run
Time: 11:15:29
Swim split: 1:10:23
Transition one: 6:40
Bike split: 5:32:50
Transition two: 5:56
Run split: 4:19:41
Age group: 1st
Place: 33rd
Racers: 218

Notes: Marjorie has a house in Cambridge, Maryland, so I decided to jump into the nearby Ironman-distance race. Race-day logistics never were as simple. My stress level was at an all-time low pre-race, until the zipper on my wetsuit broke at the start. I asked someone to duct tape it shut. I spun around. They held the tape. I looked mummified. People stared and laughed. This would be my last race in my trusty Quintana Roo wetsuit.

The duct tape was too tight. During the swim, it constricted my breathing, as my lungs couldn't expand fully. Little water entered my wetsuit though. My swim-transition time increased dramatically, while I spun around again, as someone held the end of the duct tape. The unwinding caused dizziness. I rode off with my head spinning.

The bike course goes through a marshy area. It's hot, humid, and windy. While visiting Marjorie, I'd trained on the course. Knowing the course was a tremendous benefit. I ran the entire marathon with no walking. Marjorie's support helped greatly. I won my age group. She greeted me at the finish. If I hadn't spent so much time in transition, I might have broken 11 hours. Since I won my age group by a significant margin, I was satisfied with my performance.

This race is now Ironman Maryland.

17. <u>Ironman Taiwan:</u>
Penghu Islands, Taiwan

Date: October 2, 2016
My age: 55
Distances: 2.4-mile swim, 112-mile bike, 26.2-mile run
Time: 13:59:14
Swim split: 1:02:13
Bike split: 5:48:41
Run split: 6:51:41
Transitions: 16:37
Age group: 1st (swim), 1st (bike), 5th overall
Place: 315th
Racers: 1,600

Notes: I hadn't raced a triathlon for five years. I prepared extremely well for this event and again had the goal of breaking ten hours. Until I arrived in the Penghu Islands, I didn't realize the course is so hilly. I confused this race with a different flatter Ironman-distance race in Taiwan. I accidentally entered the wrong race. I expected a flat and fast bike course. There was nothing I could do about the more difficult course now.

Airplanes can accommodate only so many bikes and with nearly everyone coming to the Penghu Islands being a triathlete, some bikes wouldn't fit. In anticipation of this problem, I employed a special bike-transportation service. For a few hundred dollars, they guaranteed my bicycle would be there several days before the race. My bike didn't show up at the promised time. I worried. My bike arrived at the eleventh hour. I rushed to assemble it to meet the deadline for bike drop off.

This was the inaugural event for Ironman Taiwan. They were working through logistical issues. The swim start was well organized. In the Strait of Taiwan, I pushed the swim and came out of the water near the front of the pack. I hammered the first half of the bike in 2:30. I was on pace. The problem was that the heat index reached 115°F, and already by mile 40 my legs were cramping. This was a bad omen.

What happened next was totally unexpected. At the aid stations, the organizers ran out of supplies and fluids. On the multi-loop course, there were crowds of racers lining up to obtain water. Due to this issue, I slowed dramatically during the second part of the bike segment. I would have slowed anyway, but severe dehydration exacerbated my problems. Although the organizers tried to solve the logistical nightmare, they weren't able to do so in real-time. I suffered, as did other competitors.

I made the mistake of wearing my $350 aero helmet. Due to its aerodynamic advantage, in theory this helmet would save me two minutes over a five-hour ride. The helmet has no vents. Although intended to save me time, the helmet ended up costing me about 20 minutes. Inside the helmet turned oven, my head felt like it was going to explode. I should have used my non-aero helmet, which has plenty of vents, and would have allowed me to get airflow and cooling on my head.

Because I was covered in salt, badly dehydrated, and overheated, in an effort to recover, I soft pedaled the last ten miles of the bike. My plan didn't work. I'd been without fluids far too long. I went too deep. The tank was empty. When I reached the second transition area, I could hear Kig cheering. I managed a smile. She may have thought that I was going to finish in the top-ten overall, but I knew better. I might not finish at all.

While sitting in the blazing sun, thinking about my next move, I noticed there were almost no bikes around. I was near the top of the leaderboard. However, I was cramping too much to think about putting on my running shoes. I put on sunblock instead. I sat there for ten minutes eating and drinking. The smart thing to do would have been to drop out. I couldn't run the marathon. I would be risking my health to continue. But, because Kig had traveled to the race to support me, I wanted to finish.

During the run, I wasn't competing. I felt horrendous. I was surviving. I ended up going to the bathroom about every two miles. My stomach problems were caused by the extreme heat and my poor intake of fluids. The expensive trisuit, which I was racing in for the first time, was designed to be worn throughout the race. In theory it would save me transition time because I wouldn't need to change clothes.

The trisuit ended up costing me at least half an hour. I had to remove it to go to the bathroom. Shorts could have been pulled down, but the one-piece trisuit had to come off my shoulders. Modern trisuits have solved this problem with a slit in the front. The actual temperatures on race day were much higher than forecast, and I paid the price for poor gear selections, regarding my aero helmet and trisuit.

I ended up walking most of the marathon. Amazingly, I still finished 5th in my age group. I wasn't there to collect my award. My "run" time was longer than my swim and bike times combined. This was by far my slowest Ironman to date. I'm confident that if I'd ridden conservatively and not had a sub-10 hour goal, I could have finished in around 11 hours and probably won my age group. I would have qualified for the Ironman World Championships, but it wasn't to be.

My plan was flawed; my gear selections wrong. Coupled with the race organizer's mistakes, I had no chance of meeting my goal. I emptied the tank, but on a day when many professional athletes dropped out, I couldn't have broken ten hours. It wasn't in the cards. Under the circumstances, if I hadn't entered the race in great shape, I wouldn't have even finished. Kig met me at the finish. I was glad that I persisted.

18. Swissman Extreme Triathlon:
Ascona, Switzerland

Date: June 24, 2017
My age: 55
Distances: 2.4-mile swim, 112-mile bike, 26.2-mile run
Climbing: 17,500 feet (approximate)
Time: 17:47:00
Swim split: 1:04:00
Transition one: 12:00
Bike split: 9:00:00
Transition two: 25:00
Run split: 7:06:00
Racers: 250

Notes: The race organizers screen entries. Due to the narrow roads and demanding nature of the course, the field is limited to 250 experienced athletes. I felt lucky to receive an entry. My goal in this race was to finish. I didn't have a specific-time goal. Anything under the cutoff would be fine. Due to the amount of climbing, my preparation included dieting.

For the start I woke up at 2:00 AM. At 4:00 AM all athletes are required to board a boat. It ferried us out to the middle of Lake Ascona for the 5:00 AM start. When we jumped off the boat, it was still dark. Although in great swimming shape, I took it easy. While trying to chart a straight course to the light at the swim exit, which was initially 2.4 miles away, I looked up frequently in the darkness. As I exited the water, my team cheered. I wanted a stress-free transition, so I took my time getting out of my wetsuit. I methodically changed into my cycling gear.

My crew consisted of Shagg, Diana, and Kig. They did a wonderful job. I'd prepared properly for the bike and done rides in Thailand having an incredible amount of steep climbing. When I descended the first mountain pass though, I noticed a loose headset. My bicycle wobbled badly, but I regained control. I didn't want to worry my crew, so I didn't mention the problem to them. They handed me drinks and gels from our SUV. They smiled and cheered, enjoying the race and the scenery of the high, snowy Swiss Alps.

Throughout the bike segment, I feathered my brakes on descents and couldn't descend full gas. Although I almost never got passed going uphill, I frequently got passed going downhill. I worried about my safety. There were two fatal accidents on the bike course, where I was significantly delayed. The people who died weren't affiliated with the race, but one of them was cycling in a tunnel that I needed to transit. After a long delay, where race officials stopped riders, I walked over the dead man's blood to get through the tunnel. Riding wasn't permitted. The loss of life made me sick.

Shagg learned that ahead they wouldn't be able to support me because of blocked roads caused by the accidents. The police weren't letting vehicles through the tunnels. With 37 miles remaining on the bike, I needed to carry a backpack with my running gear and any supplies that I could manage. I received no support for the remainder of the bike course. I didn't know when I would meet my crew next.

In the bike-to-run transition area, I spent about 25 minutes telephoning my crew and instructing them where to pick up my bicycle. There are no bike racks in this race, as normally the rider hands the bike off directly to a crew member. However, in this case most crews weren't able to get to the bike-to-run transition ahead of their athletes.

Before ending our call, my enthusiastic crew gave me valuable words of encouragement. I remained positive. We hoped for the best and a quick rendezvous. A number of triathletes whom I spoke to planned to drop out at T2 because they didn't have their running shoes. I was lucky Shagg found out about the crewing problem early. When I set off on the run, I left my cycling gear and bicycle unattended. After struggling to get going and a few painful strides, my concern about gear quickly vanished. I focused on running the brutal course.

My team finally caught up to me at mile 16 of the mountainous run course. Without support for five hours, I bonked. I was deeply relieved to see my crew, and vice versa. I ate and drank like a wild man. Unable to exercise any self-restraint, I over did it. Kig ran with me for the next few miles. From there Shagg took over pacing duties. He felt relieved to get out from behind the SUV's wheel. The drive was intense. For the final climb up to the high-altitude Kleiner Scheidegg, pacers are mandatory. Shagg and I carried required survival gear.

I reached the finish line with Shagg. We hugged and smiled. I tried to jump. Shagg did. I finished well within the original time limit. Similar to my case, many racers were delayed for a couple hours and had to carry on without support. Race organizers extended the cutoff. There were seven entrants as old as me, four of them finished. The closest one to me was 54 minutes behind. In a sense I won my age group. At the Swissman the organizers don't keep track of placings. Finishing itself is a badge of honor.

After many trials and tribulations, Kig and Diana made it to the finish line. Unfortunately, they arrived after us. We were ecstatic to see them. We exchanged smiles and strong hugs. On a truly spectacular course, it was an epic day for everyone. The course is considered by many to be the hardest Ironman-distance race in the world. I tend to agree. I said: "I won't be doing that again."

Although a beautiful race, the course was open to traffic. The steep, narrow roads are simply too dangerous for me to race on—especially with a damaged headset. After the race we toured in the Swiss Alps and then went to Paris for much deserved R&R. I then headed to Slovenia to meet Fiddlehead for our upcoming hike of the Via Dinarica. Shagg joined me for several days. Diana returned to the US, and Kig to Thailand.

19. Laguna Phuket Triathlon:
Phuket, Thailand

Date: November 22, 2020
My age: 59
Distances: 1.8K swim, 51K bike, 12K run
Time: 3:20:56
Swim split one: 23:22 (1.25K ocean)
Run between and swim split two: 10:29 (.55K lagoon)
Total swim: 33:51
Bike split: 1:36:47
Run split: 1:04:30
Transition one: 3:18
Transition two: 2:30
Age group: 1st (swim), 1st (bike), 1st overall
Place: 47th
Finishers: 358

Notes: This is the oldest and most competitive triathlon in Asia. The bike course is technical and has steep gradients over 20%. In the tropical jungle, moss has turned the roads green. The asphalt behaves like ice when wet. It was critical to preview the course. During the race, the roads aren't closed to automobile traffic. You can't swing wide on any of the hairpins. Although some competitors rode their TT bikes, for safety I chose my road bike.

I completed my 4,556-mile epic ride around Thailand a month before the race. I was in incredible cycling shape. I entered at this tri at the last minute though, and I hadn't done *any* run training. For that reason I held back on the bike. Normally one would need to enter this race on the day entries opened, almost a year earlier, but because of the COVID-19 situation, I was able to get a late entry.

On race day the heat index reached 100°F. I swam well and felt good coming off the bike. I hung tough on the run. The skies opened up after the race. The violent storm cancelled the last half of the awards ceremony, and I was disappointed not to receive my trophy on stage. The bike-to-run transition and run-finish areas are in two separate locations. My GPS unit, which was on my bike, died from getting soaked. The race had excellent organization, and the COVID-19 protocols worked well. All racers wore masks to check-in, the pre-race meeting, body marking, and the start.

Due to COVID-19 issues and the lack of tourists in Phuket, I was able to rent a beautiful condo in Laguna cheaply. If I can gain race entry again, when I'm in good shape for all three disciplines, I would like to return. The beautiful-beach start in Phuket, the unique nature of the two-segment swim, the technical circuit, the steep hills on the bike course, and the hilly, winding run make for a wonderful adventure. The heat and humidity guarantee challenging conditions.

10. Swimming

"Six more loops? You told me two to go last time!"

When I was a teenager, Fish asked me to join a swim team. We worked out five days per week. I enjoyed the camaraderie and training. I competed in swim meets. While in graduate school in Seattle, I joined a Masters Swim team. We swam at the Helene Madison Pool. She won three Olympic-gold medals and set 20 world records. My coach Robin was excellent. While swimming competitively in college, she qualified for the NCAA championships in *every* event.

Robin gave me stroke instruction: "Keep your elbow high," "Pretend you're taking your hand out of a suitcoat," and "Push the water past your hip." Her workouts were well structured. We had some good swimmers on the team. They pushed me hard in practice. The only problem was the workouts started at 5:00 AM. I needed to be in bed by 8:00 PM to wake up at 4:00 AM. I disciplined myself.

Occasionally, two of the best synchronized swimmers in the world, Olympic-gold medalists Tracie Ruiz and Candy Costie, would join us. Their sculling techniques were flawless. I watched and learned. Robin encouraged me to compete in Masters Swim meets. I did but the primary reason I joined the team was to improve for triathlon. I improved a lot while swimming with Robin. I went to various lakes to train for open-water swimming. In Seattle's Green Lake, a rowing coach scolded me for taking up too much space in the lake. I didn't respond. I kept swimming.

When I moved to New Hampshire, I trained in Dover in what's now the Jenny Thompson Pool. She won 12 Olympics medals, including eight golds, and set 15 world records. Her coaches Mike and Amy Parratto coached my Masters Swim team. I swam with Amy. Mike was the best coach I ever had. He's a well-known and widely decorated coach. Mike has a demeanor that makes you want to achieve whatever he asks. I improved under his tutelage. I wish that I'd had the opportunity to train with him at a younger age.

I once swam a set of 100s with Jenny. It was my fastest set ever. It was ten 100s on 1:10. The 70 seconds included the time for swimming and resting. The faster you swam, the more rest you got, but of course, the more fatigued you were from the harder effort. I swam freestyle while Jenny only kicked! Her feet were propellers, putting out a huge wash. I tried to surf her wake. She came in ahead of me on every 100. While she chatted with Mike after each interval, I gasped for air for five seconds, before starting the next swim.

I entered more swim meets. I trained with professors at the University of New Hampshire. Sometimes Bill Reeves, one of the top triathletes in New England, would train with us. When I moved to Savannah, I bought a house with a pool. When I moved to Annapolis, I trained in the Naval Academy's 50-meter pool. I shared a lane with Midshipmen, and we completed tough workouts. Their triathlon-team's members swam three abreast in a lane to simulate the crowded conditions of a triathlon. When I bought a condo, I made sure there was a good pool for working out. Whenever Fish and I got together, we worked in a swim. I swam regularly. Before each triathlon competition, I ramped up my training.

I wanted to enter a marathon swim, and I trained for a 10K. I completed that in the warm waters of Sattahip, Thailand. I hope to be able to compete in more long-distance swims, once the COVID-19 pandemic subsides. Although I might not be able to run as much as I grow older, I see swimming as a sport that I can continue for many years to come. Swimming provides a great overall workout, and you don't experience the same pounding as you do from running. Running tends to tighten muscles and reduce flexibility, whereas swimming does the opposite.

I didn't maintain records for my races at swimming meets. At Robin's urging, I remember competing in the "animal meet," which consisted of a 200 butterfly, a 400 individual medley, and a 1,650 freestyle. I do have the records for my PRs at 500 and 1,650 yards and for my 10K swim. If I enter any more events, I'll keep better records. I list my swims for which I have data.

- 500 PR:
  Seattle, Washington

  Date: October 3, 1988
  My age: 27
  Distance: 500 yards
  Time: 5:26

- 1650 PR:
  Seattle, Washington

  Date: October 5, 1988
  My age: 27
  Distance: 1,650 yards
  Time: 19:27

Notes: Of the 65 swimmers entered in the race, I was seeded eighth. My heat contained the fastest eight swimmers. I remember gasping for breath after 500 yards. I couldn't get in enough oxygen. My body tensed. Each time I turned my head sideways, I opened my mouth widely and sucked in as much air as possible. Robin walked alongside my lane, swinging a towel overhead and shouting encouragement. She motivated me.

There was no way I could compete with the recent graduates who swam competitively in college. Robin saw that I gave as much effort though. I could barely get out of the pool. My entire body was red, especially my cheeks. I had gone full gas and emptied the tank. Robin was proud of me. Although I finished dead last in my heat, she made me feel like a champion. I finished in the top-ten overall.

- Thailand Swimathon:
  Sattahip, Thailand

Date: December 2, 2017
My age: 56
Distance: 10K
Time: 3:06:50
Age group (40 and older): 3rd
Place: 12th
Racers: 146

Notes: We ran into the water from a mass beach start, but there were far fewer competitors than in the triathlons that I'd raced. The swimmers were more polite and relaxed than triathletes, too. I felt safer. Pre-race I was told the 10K involved five loops of the two-kilometer course. I never checked my watch. I counted my loops. After four loops, relishing in the fact that I had only one more to go, I was informed I needed to complete another six loops. The course was only one kilometer in length, not two. I wasn't even halfway.

After the crushing disappointment, I nearly dropped out. I slowed my stroke rate and reduced my kick. At the conclusion of each loop, there was a beach run to the entry point for the next loop. I never saw a clock. Because of the warm water and hot air, while in full stride on the beach, I guzzled water and an electrolyte beverage to replace what was lost. I took some gels.

Other than the problem with counting loops, I enjoyed the race and the camaraderie among the swimmers. After competing it was nice not to experience severe soreness, as I always did in long-distance running events and triathlons. My shoulders and arms quickly recovered.

11. Scuba Diving

"You mean jump in there? You go first."

In this chapter I list items related to scuba diving and snorkeling. I should point out that *Scuba* stands for Self-Contained Underwater Breathing Apparatus. *PADI* stands for the Professional Association of Diving Instructors; *NAUI* stands for the National Association of Underwater Instructors; *SSI* stands for Scuba Schools International. *BCD* stands for buoyancy control device. I make use of these diving acronyms here.

I completed my first-ever dive from a beach entry in Rhode Island. My brother Rob dressed me in a BCD and weight belt. While handing me a regulator, he said: "Here, breathe normally through this." Of course at that time, I didn't know what a regulator was. I followed his instruction. There was only one. It was a solo dive. We only had one set of gear. Luckily I survived. Tarman got me into organized scuba diving. I was certified in beautiful Turks and Caicos. The PADI course focused on safe diving. When I dove "with" my brother, I never realized all the things that could go wrong. As of this writing, I logged 338 dives.

I dove in many different conditions: cold water, low visibility, strong currents, rough seas, and so forth. I dove with many different divers from all over the world, having a wide range of experience. I dove/snorkeled with many different creatures, including sharks on feeding dives at Stuart's Cove in the Bahamas, manta rays in Yap, thresher sharks in the Philippines, whale sharks in Thailand, seals and marine iguanas in the Galapagos, giant clams in Australia's Great Barrier Reef, and big sharks in the Gulf Stream. I dove with all sorts of different entries from jumping off rocks on Bonaire's shore to squeezing into caves and cenotes in Mexico to rolling out of bamboo-made catamarans in the Philippines to swimming through cracks leading to springs in Florida.

I dove at all hours of the day and night. I dove on a wide variety of dive sites. I dove fresh-water lakes. I dove on and penetrated many wrecks, including commercial aircraft, fighter planes, warships, helicopters, submarines, cargo ships, pirate ships, ancient sailing vessels, ferries, and scuttled ships. I dove many sites that are considered to be in the top-ten dive sites in the world, places such as the Blue Corner in Palau, the Great Blue Hole in Belize, and Richelieu Rock in the Andaman Sea. My Mount Everest of diving is Chuuk Lagoon. The deepest I dove is 185 feet.

Tarman and I completed many diving certifications together. The majority of courses were taken in remote, exotic diving locations. Most scuba certifications involve course work, land-based training, and diving. Some require a completion of a certain number of dives before attaining a given level. Less-involved courses can sometimes be completed in a day. Others may require weeks.

A good diver learns new tricks of the trade constantly. Equipment and techniques evolve. It's important to remain current. I try to dive on a regular basis. I start off by providing a list of my diving certifications. Following this I provide a list of my diving/snorkeling locations. Many of these are remote, and they involve extensive travel to get there, for example, Reunion Island, Micronesia, Vanuatu, and the Maldives.

When I review the list of sites, I see that I spent about two full years of my life on diving trips, meaning 730 days. In other words for someone to follow in my footsteps and visit all these locations, if they were dedicated full-time to this pursuit, they would require two entire years. If it weren't for diving I probably wouldn't have visited some of these locations. Diving opened up many new adventures and opportunities.

From most-to-least recent, the following is a list of my scuba-diving certifications.

1. PADI Wreck Diver
2. PADI Dive Instructor
3. PADI Specialist Instructor (SI) as Oxygen Provider
4. PADI SI for Project Aware
5. PADI SI for Project Aware: Coral Reef
6. PADI SI for Peak Performance Buoyancy
7. PADI SI for Nitrox
8. Emergency First Responder
9. Instructor for Emergency First Responder
10. NAUI Dive Master
11. SSI Master Diver
12. SSI Rescue Diver
13. SSI Advanced Open Water Diver
14. SSI Deep Diving
15. SSI Underwater Navigation
16. SSI Nitrox
17. SSI Underwater Photography
18. PADI Open Water

The list of certifications shows that I'm a NAUI Dive Master but became a PADI Dive Instructor. The conversion from the NAUI to the PADI system was a real challenge. I learned the SSI, NAUI, and PADI systems, which gives me a greater depth of knowledge. However, I had to fill in many gaps along the way, as the systems don't follow the same methods and styles. This path was challenging, especially because I never worked as a dive professional.

In what follows I organized my diving and snorkeling locations alphabetically by continent. In most of these places, I visited numerous locations and dive sites.

Africa:
- Egypt (Sharm El Sheik)
- Reunion Island
- South Africa

Asia:

- Bahrain
- Georgia
- Indonesia (Bali)
- Kazakhstan
- Kyrgyzstan
- Maldives
- Oman
- Philippines (Bohol, Boracay, Cebu, Dukit, Gato, Leyte, Mala-papsuca, Negros, Palawan, Panglao, Siquijor, and Tubbatha)
- Sri Lanka
- Thailand (Koh Bayu, Koh Bon, Koh Chang, Koh Ha, Koh Hin Pousar, Koh Kai, Koh Klang, Koh Lanta, Koh Miang, Koh Nang Yuan, Koh Payu, Koh Ri, Koh Samui, Koh Similian, Koh Surin Nuea, Koh Surin Tai, Koh Tao, Koh Tachai, Krabi, Phuket, Similian Islands, and Surin Islands)
- Turkmenistan

Europe:
- Croatia
- Cyprus
- Greece
- Italy
- Romania
- Switzerland

North America:
- Antigua and Barbuda
- Bahamas (Freeport and Nassau)
- Barbados
- Belize
- Bermuda
- California
- Dominican Republic

- Florida (Boynton Beach, Ginny Springs, many locations in the Keys, and West Palm)
- Grand Cayman
- Grenada
- Hawaii (Kauai and Oahu)
- Jamaica
- Maine
- Maryland
- Massachusetts
- Mexico (Baja, Cancun, Cozumel, Pinto Point, and Yucatan)
- New Hampshire
- North Carolina
- Oregon
- Rhode Island
- St. Lucia
- St. Maarten
- St. Thomas
- Saint Vincent and the Grenadines
- South Carolina
- Tobago
- Turks and Caicos
- US Virgin Islands
- Virginia
- Washington

Oceania:
- Australia (Great Barrier Reef)
- Chuuk (see Truk below)
- Cook Islands
- Federated States of Micronesia
- Fiji
- Guam
- New Caledonia

- New Zealand
- Palau
- Truk/Chuuk: engine-room penetrations on the Heian Maru, Kensho Maru, Nippo Maru, Shinkoku Maru, and Yamagiri Maru. San Francisco Maru.
- Vanuatu
- West Carolines
- Yap

South America:
- Aruba
- Bonaire
- Brazil
- Columbia
- Galapagos

I still have many diving goals to fulfill. The most immediate ones are to dive in the Solomon Islands and Ningaloo Reef in Western Australia. As of this writing, the COVID-19 pandemic has put my travel on hold.

12. DNFs

"That's it for today."

As of this writing, my palmarès lists 148 competitions. In this chapter I discuss the seven events, where I was a DNF (Did Not Finish). In the case of solo RAAM 2013, I completed the race but was listed as an unofficial finisher. In the 12-day event, the cutoff beat me by a small margin. Overall I completed 96% (142/148) of the events that I started.

In a number of activities which I finished, I suffered substantial adversity: I crashed and injured myself and damaged my bicycle; I got struck by lightning; I became sick with vomiting and/or diarrhea; I got lost; I sustained foot trauma; I couldn't see; I experienced heat stroke; and I lost toenails. For my DNFs I discuss each in turn and explain what happened. I comment on what it meant and what I learned.

1. Leadville Trail 100:
    Leadville, Colorado

    Date: August 15, 1992
    My age: 31
    Distance: 100 miles
    Time: DNF, dropped out at Twin Lakes, 61 miles in 15:19:10

    Notes: In hindsight, I wasn't properly acclimatized for this high-altitude race. I went directly from sea level to Leadville (10,152 feet). The race reaches an altitude of 12,600 feet. I competed un-supported. After my successful run at the Western States 100, I thought I could push the pace at Leadville. I reached the midway point at Winfield in 9:41 in fifth place. I was ravenous. I ate too much. My blood went to my stomach. My muscles received insufficient oxygen. The higher I went, the more nauseous I became. I dragged myself over Hope Pass at 12,600 feet. I vomited the entire way to mile 61.

When I arrived at Twin Lakes, I felt weak. It was dark. Because I thought I would arrive much sooner, I hadn't packed any flashlights in my drop bag or any warm clothes to combat the nighttime temperatures. Without lights or sufficient clothing, I feared heading into the dark mountains alone. After a painful debate with myself, I decided to quit. I reported to a race official. With a snip of his scissors, my race ended, as my wristband fell to the ground. I hung my head.

To make a long story short, I felt like a failure. I was ashamed of myself. I never had given up. This was the first time I voluntarily quit an activity. I cried. My emotions ran amok. The bad feelings stayed with me for months. I'd let myself down. Looking back though, I made the right decision. I would have endangered myself, and perhaps others, by continuing in my weakened and ill-equipped state.

The following year I returned and completed the course in an excellent time of 23 hours. I was one of the top finishers who lived at sea level. Although I felt redeemed, thirty years later, it still hurts to know I quit in my first attempt. I failed to achieve my goal. The Leadville Trail 100 taught me a lot about myself. It forced me to grow.

2.   Angeles Crest 100 Mile Endurance Run:
     Wrightwood, California

Date: October 9, 1993
My age: 32
Distance: 100 miles
Time: DNF, dropped out at Chantry Flats, 76 miles in 17:11:00

Notes: After my excellent run at the Leadville Trail 100 less than two months earlier, I went all in at this race. I decided to go for the win. For the first 30 miles, as I mentioned previously, I ran with the leader Fred Schufflebarger. He was an excellent trail runner. When I needed to go number two, Fred disappeared. I got lost. I worried. I slowed, hoping to join up with the third-place runner. He was nowhere near us.

The race is run at altitude, and around 50 miles into the event, I started vomiting. I continued running. I stopped. I sat on the trail for an hour to try and recover. It was too late. I arrived at Chantry Flats in a good time and in the top-ten overall. I had no pacers, but my roommate from college Jimbo was there. We talked. He boosted my spirits. I removed a bunch of toenails. During daylight hours, I'd been lost frequently. In my exhausted state, Jimbo talked sense into me. I decided not to head off into darkness on an unknown trail alone.

Jimbo and I drove to the Rose Bowl. As runners finished, they asked me what happened. I explained that I DNFed. I didn't feel good talking about it. I struggled to confront my defeat. However, unlike my DNF at Leadville, I knew right away that I'd made the correct decision. I pushed myself past my limit in the first 76 miles, through the desert, up and down mountains, getting dehydrated, losing my way, and destroying my feet. Fred went on to win.

Ben Hian, another guy I ran with during the race, went on to win it four times. He set some of the fastest times ever on the course. He defeated runners like Scott Jurek. Ben holds four of the ten fastest times ever run at the Angeles Crest 100. Back then, I didn't realize I was up against the very best who would ever run this race—some of the best ultra-runners of all-time. I'd held myself to a much higher standard than I realized.

In hindsight, I could have finished the race. I had 13 hours to cover 24 miles. I didn't want a simple finish. I wanted to win, or at least to run strongly for the entire distance. I didn't want to shuffle in the last 24 miles. I gave everything I had. The all-time greats pushed me past my breaking point. Although disappointed, I wasn't crushed. I returned seven years later with the goal of finishing the race. I lowered my expectations. I paced myself sensibly. I finished. I didn't suffer as much. I felt redeemed.

3. Wasatch Front 100:
    East Layton, Utah

    Date: September 6, 1997
    My age: 36
    Distance: 100 miles
    Time: DNF, dropped out at Upper Big Water, 59.2 miles in 13:15:00

    Notes: Although in the best climbing shape of my life, just three days before the race, I caught a cold. I should have withdrawn from the race, but I didn't want to let my crew down. I went as far as I could, as fast as I could. When I decided to DNF, Tarman was with me. We talked. My emotions went berserk. He provided support. We decided I shouldn't continue.

    The DNF hurt. I cried uncontrollably. Given how sick I was, it was the right decision. It bothered me to quit. I was in tremendous shape. I didn't want Tarman to see me quit. Although I wasn't anywhere near the same level of conditioning, I came back two years later and completed the race. Being healthy and proper pacing were the keys to my redemption.

4. Ironman Arizona:
    Tempe, Arizona

    Date: November 23, 2008
    My age: 47
    Distances: 2.4-mile swim, 112-mile bike, 26.2-mile run

    Notes: I described the ordeal of this race in the chapter on triathlons. I'd set an unrealistic time goal. I didn't eat or drink properly on the bike. I lost too much salt on the run, and I didn't listen to my body. In fact I intentionally ignored my body's warnings. I didn't want to walk the last eight miles. I'd come to race, to set a good time. I didn't feel like I was quitting. I felt more like I'd given my all. I didn't feel like a failure. I was disappointed with my DNF, but I accepted it.

5. Adirondack 540:
   Wilmington, New York

   Dates: September 13-15, 2012
   My age: 51
   Distance: 544 miles

   Notes: I broke a shift lever at mile 365. It couldn't be repaired. I didn't have a crew or a spare bike. Due to the mechanical, I needed to drop out. I had no choice, as there was no bike for me to ride. I was disappointed, but I wasn't disappointed in myself. I felt fine and healthy. I could have ridden to the finish. The following year I returned and won.

6. Race Across America (RAAM):
   Oceanside, California to Annapolis, Maryland

   Dates: June 12-23, 2013
   My age: 51
   Distance: 2,962 miles

   Notes: As I noted in the chapter on cycling races, I finished over the time limit. I gave my all. I was satisfied with my effort. There were things that my crew and I could have done differently, which would have saved a few hours, but given the circumstances, I was proud of my ride. It represented one of my greatest athletic achievements. I overcame tremendous adversity. I didn't quit. I went back the following year. Although I wasn't in as good shape, I completed a longer course within the time limit.

7. Adirondack 540:
   Wilmington, New York

Dates: September 12-14, 2014
My age: 53
Distance: 544 miles

Notes: I expected to win this race, as I'd done the previous year. At mile 227 when I lost my vision, I was leading comfortably. Although I tried to recover my eyesight, I couldn't. I felt frustrated. I needed to DNF. With the low temperatures and high humidity, lenses fog up easily on this course. Even if I didn't need corrective lenses, I always wore protective lenses while riding. I didn't anticipate the severity of my eye problems, but perhaps putting eye drops in regularly would have delayed their onset and allowed me to continue. Goggles rather than glasses may have helped.

I used to fear not completing a race, not being strong enough to endure. After my DNF at the Leadville Trail 100, I went hard on myself. I learned that I sometimes pushed myself harder than is healthy. I race hard. When striving for top results, I went beyond my limits. This helped me to understand my boundaries. My goals occasionally exceeded my capabilities. This taught me to live with disappointment. I set more realistic goals. My fears of a DNF subsided. I give my all.

From my experiences I make good decisions about when to drop-out. I'm not afraid to quit. I don't give up easily. Every race, which I ever quit, I went back and completed, except Ironman Arizona. I went on to complete much harder Ironman races though. Where I failed previously, my experience helped the second time around. It also helped that I lowered my expectations. During repeats, I paced myself to a reasonable finish.

My DNFs taught me a lot. They helped me grow. My overall finishing percentage of 96 is much higher than race averages. In my toughest races, the finishing rate is about 33%. In such races only the best, most experienced and well-prepared athletes compete. Many events require one to qualify. The dropout rate is 67% versus my rate of 4%.

I focus on what I'm doing. When I worried about competing against the best, I pushed myself to the edge. If you want to be a champion, you must beat the best. Even the greatest athletes in the world have off days, make mistakes, get misdirected by officials or crew, suffer mechanicals, and end up with DNFs. It's remarkable that I never dropped out of an event due to an injury.

Once I parked my fear of failure, it allowed me to continue to dream big. My energy goes into being successful rather than fearing failure. Failing at a difficult challenge brings me more rewards than succeeding at an easy task. The process of preparing and training for a worthy objective are what I enjoy. The unknown requires anticipation. I thrive on events that combine both mental and physical abilities. I find endurance races to be such activities, as are sports such as scuba diving, mountaineering, rock climbing, and orienteering.

13. Best Experiences

"That thing belongs in the Smithsonian!"

When I was 11 years old, I started training. No one pushed me; I pushed myself. I wouldn't have continued for the past 50 years if I didn't enjoy it. I'm someone who likes being outdoors. Exercising makes me feel good. I experience endorphin highs, but they're rare. Once every two months, I have a great workout, where I'm smiling and feeling invincible. The memories of such good feelings last. They're something you want to replicate. Exercising helps me relax and reduces my stress. I enjoy the activities and process. There are many health benefits.

In this chapter I list my top-ten best athletic experiences and provide a few notes about why I enjoyed them. More details can be found in the corresponding chapters. They're not ranked but rather listed in chronological order. It was difficult to choose only ten.

1. Sunmart Texas Trail 50:
   Huntsville, Texas

   Date: December 15, 1990
   My age: 29

   Notes: This is the first ultra-marathon that I ran. Prior to this race, I wasn't sure that I *could* run nonstop for 50 miles. Finishing in third place gave me confidence in my physical ability and mental strength. I traveled to the race alone. It was one of the first trips that I planned in order to compete in an athletic event. I enjoyed the planning process and the sense of adventure. I flew to Houston from Savannah. I enjoyed sightseeing in Houston, and I made a number of new friends at the race. I found a new activity that I wanted to pursue. The race taught me a lot about myself and my limits.

2. Mount Elbrus:
   Russia, Europe

   Summit date: July 24, 2001
   My age: 39
   Elevation: 18,481 feet
   Partner: Paul Göransson

   Notes: Because I grew up during the Cold War, Russia fascinated me. Only one person I knew, Aceman, had been there. This trip was to climb the first of the seven summits, so it was the start of a multi-year adventure. There were many unknowns. Succeeding on the climb by reaching a much higher elevation than ever before, and sharing the journey with Tarman, made for an awesome experience. I learned a great deal of information firsthand, dispelling many myths propagated by those who had never been to Russia.

   This trip opened my eyes to the way the world actually is rather than how others perceive and report about it. I gained a deep understanding about propaganda, the media, and politics. From a cultural perspective, the trip broadened my horizons. I felt more positive about humanity and that's something beautiful. I wanted to keep climbing and exploring the world, seeing things for myself and forming my own opinions, while using my new and improved filter.

3. Mount Kilimanjaro:
   Tanzania, Africa

   Summit date: August 3, 2002
   My age: 41
   Elevation: 19,339 feet

Partner: Eugene

Notes: I traveled alone on this trip. I overcame much adversity to succeed. I went from sea level to 19,339 feet in four days. The climb gave me confidence that my body functioned well at high altitude. In addition to discovering new parts of Africa, I discovered new parts of myself. I satisfied my fascination with archeology by taking a trip to Olduvai Gorge. The visit to this paleoanthropological site brought me closer to our ancestors. My safaris and trip to the Ngorongoro Crater connected me closer to the animal kingdom. The journey made me feel happy to be alive and strengthened my desire to see and do more.

4. Atlanta Marathon:
   Atlanta, Georgia

   Date: November 27, 2003
   My age: 42

   Notes: I was on a very good day. It wasn't often that I negative split a marathon or felt as strong at the end, as I did at the beginning. I surged through the field in the second half of the race and ran an age-graded time of 2:47:54. Thoughts of the Atlanta Olympic Games filled me, as did memories of my trip to Atlanta with Fish, to start our thru-hike of the Appalachian Trail. I won the Masters division and placed sixth overall. In front of a cheering crowd, it felt good to receive my award on the podium. In a big city marathon, this was a great performance for me.

5. Crossing the USA:
   Provincetown, Massachusetts to San Diego, California

   Dates: April 28 to June 4, 2011
   My age: 49

Notes: Almost 50 years old, Fish and I planned and completed a ride across the continent. It took a journey of this magnitude to recreate the feelings of exploration that we shared as kids, when we ventured into a different neighborhood. We shared many adventures and overcame much adversity to arrive in San Diego on schedule. I imagine few get to share such a passage and celebrate 35+ years as best friends. We enjoyed each other's company and caught up on each other's lives.

It was reassuring to find out that my best friend from childhood still shared the same values and to learn that at the core neither one of us had changed. Facades aren't part of our lives. We are who we were and will continue to be. Our reminiscing created laughter. We relived parts of childhood.

Crossing the country successfully with only each other for support gave us inner confidence, as we rode ourselves into terrific shape. We discovered new things about ourselves and our country. Now that I'd ridden most of the course, RAAM seemed within my reach. The belief that I would compete in it was planted in my brain. This goal gave me clarity, purpose, and focus. Fish knew better what RAAM involved too.

6. Race Across America (RAAM):
   Oceanside, California to Annapolis, Maryland

   Dates: June 11-22, 2014
   My age: 52

   Notes: I took on the "World's Toughest Cycling Race" and finished it. The race requires mental and physical strength and dedication. After being declared unofficial in 2013 for finishing just outside the time limit, I came back with a group of friends and students, and completed the race officially. In training I was hit by a motorcycle and broke my collarbone. I overcame much adversity. The support and love that my crew provided gave me enormous strength. I bonded deeply with them.

Taking on the ultimate personal challenge, putting myself out there, giving everything, experiencing the kindness and devotion of friends and supporters, these things built my faith in humanity. The depth and meaning of this experience are far greater than a cycling competition. To test one's willpower, courage, self-worth, values, and identity; to commit fully and have the commitment of friends; to take risks and overcome fears; to push past normal human limits; to endure great pain and suffering; to go up against Mother Nature; to confront one's demons, and the list goes on and on; but, to do all these things and more, and meet the challenges, after coming up just short the previous year, gives me an immense sense of satisfaction and a lifetime of gratification and shared memories.

7. Continental Divide Trail (CDT):
Continental Divide, USA

Dates: April 25 to August 2, 2015 (100 days)
My age: 54

Notes: The CDT is not a well-marked or popular trail. Extreme altitude, weather, and hazards are the norm. I planned this trip alone. While hiking, I walked for days at a time without seeing anyone. This trip took me into the most rugged, wild, and remote areas of the lower 48 states. I faced my fears and overcame struggles to succeed at this adventure. The communion with nature and the chance to reflect on my life in beautiful surroundings and solitude gave me deep insights into where I want to go from here. To achieve personal clarity is a wonderful feeling.

8. Diving Trip to Chuuk/Truk:
Chuuk/Truk, Federated States of Micronesia

Dates: February 26 to March 1, 2018
My age: 56

Notes: Most people haven't heard of Chuuk (also called Truk), including Japanese. Getting to the island is challenging. After reading an article confirming that the WWII wrecks there were starting to crumble, I decided to go. I studied the remote area. I learned about previous diving accidents. If something went wrong, assistance was far away. I researched the available diving options. The sites were deep. Many lost their lives in this location. The wrecks are referred to as the "Ghost fleet of Truk Lagoon."

I purchased new dive gear, including a wing BCD, a Shearouse dive computer, and a high-end regulator. Before heading off to Chuuk, I trained with the equipment in Phuket, Thailand. Tarman met me in Chuuk. His arduous travel left him with a cold, but we completed a number of dives together. We caught up at meals. With my guide Dar, I made engine-room penetrations on the Heian Maru, Kensho Maru, Nippo Maru, Shinkoku Maru, and Yamagiri Maru. In WWII the Maru suffix was used on the names of Japanese merchant ships. Some of these ships are over 500 feet in length. We dove the San Francisco Maru too.

Seventy-five years after Operation Hailstone, through a labyrinth of crumbling metal, we penetrated four-levels deep into the dark, sunken, coral-coated ships. Inside the wrecks, we encountered human bones, military tanks, unexploded ordinance, vehicles, and of course, many species of fish. I did most dives with Patrick—a fearless man who'd flown over 300 combat missions in Vietnam. We completed a wreck-diving certification course together. I learned a lot about WWII history, the people of Chuuk, and myself.

This trip required detailed planning, training, and skill. My diving expanded into a new realm. The gulf between my first dive in Rhode Island and the diving in Chuuk is huge. I never anticipated taking my diving to this level. I never dreamed of engine-room penetrations on WWII wrecks in Chuuk. It made for an unbelievably gratifying experience. The trip exceeded my expectations and dreams. To share the adventure with Tarman was amazing. I made new friends. We bonded.

Dar visited me in Thailand. I'm in touch with Patrick. When travel restrictions ease, we hope to arrange another diving trip together. Tarman plans to join us.

9. <u>Trans America Trail:</u>
Astoria, Oregon to Yorktown, Virginia

Dates: May 27 to July 8, 2018
My age: 56

Notes: After cycling unsupported across the USA with Fish, completing the RAAM course twice solo, and pedaling across Thailand dozens of times, I felt confident about riding the TAT in my home country. I cycled the route on my mountain bike. Although numerous parts challenged me, I never doubted for a moment that I would finish. My knowledge, obtained through years of experience and training, gave me the ability to adjust to any unforeseen circumstances.

Huck Lem joined me for a number of sections. Our camaraderie added to my enjoyment. Fish helped me arrange numerous accommodations. Our correspondence and his virtual participation added value. Crossing the PCT, CDT, and AT brought back memories. Riding parts of the RAAM route gave me goose bumps. My history and previous travels throughout the US made my journey incredibly rewarding, as did finishing as planned. I connected with my close friends Marjorie and Geir after the trip.

10. <u>Chiang Mai around Northern Thailand Return:</u>
Chiang Mai to 33 provinces, and return to Chiang Mai, Thailand

Dates: August 2 to October 19, 2020
My age: 59

Notes: During the COVID-19 pandemic, I completed this ride solo. This is my longest bicycle ride. Due to the lockdown in Thailand, in closed-border regions, there was no traffic. I rode 75 miles without seeing a vehicle. The ride gave me a great chance to explore in solitude. Due to the isolation and remoteness, some people may have felt concerned for their safety, whereas I felt at ease. Although riding in rainy season, the freedom of the road, especially during the pandemic, provided me a great personal reward. Due to my experience and preparation, I handled many challenges without fear or incident. The epic ride gave me a chance to reflect and count my lucky stars.

Although I provided notes about what these activities meant to me, it's worth considering common themes.

Most of the experiences selected have a duration longer than one week, many over a month, and some more than three months. Being away for a longer period allows me to immerse myself fully in an activity and disengage from routine and mundane aspects of life. This separation brings me fulfillment, as many opportunities for self-discovery and adventure arise in unfamiliar circumstances. I've made long journeys part of my "normal" life. Logistics and planning are complex. Commitment is required.

During long trips, intense learning takes place regarding self, friends, customs, cultures, history, nature, language, perceptions, cuisine, geography, and so much more. You meet many people and see many places. You're thrust into new situations and environments. When experiencing things firsthand, beliefs and knowledge are either confirmed or refuted. Change and growth take place. Challenges spanning months mean facing greater adversity and developing better problem-solving skills. A long duration means there's a necessity for innovation and a time for reflection. Wisdom is increased.

The activities listed in this chapter were completed at the ages of 29, 39, 41, 42, 49, 52, 54, 56 (two items), and 59. With age I had more freedom and time to explore. I arranged my life that way. I looked beyond my backyard, beyond the US's borders. I could go anywhere in the world, and I became selective in choosing what to pursue. I understood the world and myself better, so if I chose carefully, I could find worthwhile activities that I would benefit from and enjoy more.

Because I understood myself better, I chose things that made me happier. I shared deeper, longer, and more meaningful friendships. For the most part, my friends had more flexibility, resources, and ability to travel. We shared in bigger adventures. I realized what combination of physical and mental stimulation satisfied me. I learned about new challenges and opportunities from fellow travelers. They enhanced my journey. The Internet provided a forum to learn about new activities and see images of nearly any faraway place. The digital world facilitated research and arranging travel.

Over the years through much sweat, I developed confidence in my abilities. Without self-doubt generating fear, I enjoyed myself more. There was no second guessing. I learned from my mistakes. With experience came better judgment. I reached a point where I didn't need to prove anything to myself or others. I accepted myself. It took a long time. Based on available inputs, I learned to make good, timely decisions. I trusted myself. I learned to be flexible. I learned to be patient. I learned what risks were acceptable. If something crossed my line, I didn't do it. I didn't succumb to pressure. I took full responsibility for my actions and safety.

Having constructed a wealth of memories, through many diverse experiences, I have a library to draw on to help me cope with challenging situations. This repository has reduced my fears and provided me peace of mind. When I'm at peace and in a groove, good memories flow back, and I relive favorable experiences. My imagination expands, and I form new dreams. Success does breed success. The realm of the possible expands. I exceeded my limits in a number of races, knowing where my boundaries were helped me survive solo journeys across the country and numerous worldwide expeditions. Although the possibilities are endless, no one is invincible.

In getting super fit, the mind becomes sharper. Thoughts flow naturally and efficiently. When relaxed and feeling good, things become effortless. An inexplicable clarity is reached. Once I experienced these wonderful sensations, I wanted to experience them again and again. However, I kept things in perspective and understood my limitations, and the risks involved in certain activities. Dispensing with fear completely isn't healthy. One can't always go bigger, faster, farther, and deeper.

It's worth leaving something on the table. It's worth having an unfulfilled goal—one never acted upon. It keeps us humble. That objective serves as a guiding light, stimulating our curiosity and forcing us to confront our limitations. The goal can be passed down to the next generation. It can be conquered in stages. When we let go of our focus totally, thinking we've achieved everything possible, we become complacent. We lose something.

It's okay not to probe the depth of every goal. It's okay and healthy to let an unfulfilled goal float around in the background. It leaves us striving. Humans have overcome obstacles throughout our history. It's important for our species that some of us are willing to take on difficult challenges and assume risks, to reach for the stars. When one of us achieves a breakthrough, the collective strengthens. We must evolve to continue to thrive.

14. Hardest Activities

"I won't be doing that again."

My frame of mind, fitness level, fear, age, injuries, weather, equipment, support, duration, terrain, and remoteness determine how hard I perceive something to be. The items listed in this chapter require skill, dedication, commitment, risk, and preparation, regardless of when they're done. Some honorable mentions are as follows: the Swissman Extreme Ironman, the Trans America Trail, the Wasatch Front 100, the Via Dinarica White Route, the Angeles Crest 100, and most of my 1,000+-mile bicycle rides in Thailand.

With all due respect to RAAM, the hardest thing I've ever done and intend to do was set the FKT for the PCT. To this day I consider myself lucky to be alive and admit that I took too many risks on that journey. The PCT is much safer to hike now than before it became a popular trail, especially if GPS and apps providing real-time information are utilized. With technological innovation, improved equipment, better nutrition, and more accurate information available, it's impossible to compare the difficulty of completing something in the past versus the present—summiting Mount Everest is a good example.

Because I elaborated on these activities elsewhere, I simply provide a chronological listing here. They're not listed in order of perceived difficulty.

1. Appalachian Trail (AT):
   East Coast Mountains, USA

   Distance: 2,169 miles
   Dates: May 11 to August 16, 1995 (97 days)

My age: 34

2. Aconcagua:
    Argentina, South America

    Summit date: January 9, 2002
    My age: 40

3. Pacific Crest Trail (PCT):
    West Coast Mountains, USA

    Distance: 2,659 miles
    Dates: May 12 to August 2, 2003 (83 days)
    My age: 41

4. Vinson Massif:
    Sentinel Range of the Ellsworth Mountains, Antarctica

    Summit date: January 10, 2005
    My age: 43

5. Mount McKinley:
    Alaska, North America

    Summit date: May 26, 2009
    My age: 47

6. Race Across America (RAAM):
    Oceanside, California to Annapolis, Maryland

    Dates: June 12-23, 2013
    My age: 51

7. Race Across America (RAAM):
    Oceanside, California to Annapolis, Maryland

    Dates: June 11-22, 2014

My age: 52
Distance: 3,020 miles

8. Continental Divide Trail (CDT):
    Continental Divide, USA

    Distance: 2,800 miles
    Dates: April 25 to August 2, 2015 (100 days)
    My age: 54

9. East to West Walk across Thailand:
    Ubon Ratchathani, Thailand/Laos border to Mae Hong Son, Thailand Myanmar border

    Distance: 725 miles
    Dates: March 12 to April 3, 2018 (22 days and 9 hours)
    My age: 56

10. Chiang Mai to Luang Prabang Return:
    Chiang Mai, Thailand to Luang Prabang, Laos

    Dates: April 12 to April 22, 2018
    My age: 56
    Distance: 803 miles

11. Chiang Mai to Vientiane to Lampang:
    Chiang Mai, Thailand to Vientiane, Laos

    Dates: April 28 to May 17, 2018
    My age: 56
    Distance: 1,370 miles

12. Chiang Mai around Northern Thailand Return:
    Chiang Mai to 33 provinces, and return to Chiang Mai, Thailand

    Dates: August 2 to October 19, 2020

My age: 59
Distance: 4,556 miles

15. Favorite Quotes

"I want to live my life. For me that means taking chances. I will not let fear stop me from doing things that I really want to."

This chapter includes a number of my favorite personal quotes. These are things that I said. Others may have said them too.

- To achieve personal clarity is a wonderful feeling.

- I'll decide when I get there, when I see it.

- It's only another few hundred miles.

- There's very little which I can do about that now.

- That's what she said.

- I'm not sure. We either need to go left or right. There are no other options. Pick one.

- How many insane asylums are there in Kansas?

- Are you gonna eat that?

- Go ahead. You go first.

- Yes, I did just drive around the perimeter of Australia in three weeks. It was 10,000 miles. You said unlimited mileage.

- I'm out of water.

- I have one granola bar left.

- That looks good.

- Today, everybody's an online critic—people who've never done anything and have no qualifications. They're experts.

- Yeah, I'm tired.

- No, I didn't get a vaccine. The USA gave away 500,000,000 vaccines, but expats weren't allowed to get one. We put a man on the moon over 50 years ago, so yes, the government could have provided vaccines to all its taxpayers and citizens.

- I don't know; I don't know what's going on. I care.

- What country are you from!?

- He said something about there being such and such a thing somewhere around here.

- The map shows that it should be right here. Landmarks don't just get up and walk away. The map's wrong.

- My tongue is sore as hell, and my ass is killing me (during RAAM). If I wake up feeling like that, there better be a couple hundred bucks in my pocket (Wilson's reply).

- It ain't gonna ride itself, Boy.

- The schedule was too ambitious.

- I won't be doing that again.

- I have no other information.

- I'm returning from Antarctica, where are you coming from?

- The Via Dinarica, it's not for everybody (Fiddlehead and I).

- Give me another Jelen Pivo.

- Nema problema.

- I just completed the Triple Crown.

- If that Bull Moose comes any closer, I'll blast his nostrils with this bear spray.

- The largest silverback in the world charged me to about seven feet—a 550-pound gorilla—he pounded his chest. I didn't make eye contact.

- I lost you after you said, "I think that …"

- Yes, I'm alone.

- This is probably my last Ironman (after completing Ironman Taiwan in extreme heat).

- This is probably my last Ironman (after completing the Swissman Extreme a year later).

- There's no way I'm coming off the bike. This is the first tail-wind I've had (in winds approaching hurricane force in Kansas at RAAM 2013).

- I don't know. I never really thought about it.

- Are you kidding me?

- If it's broken, fix it.

- Mom, you're the greatest!

- Are you committed to this? Can you hike 55 miles with six socks on that foot? (To Tarman after the sole of his shoe fell off halfway into the 100-mile wilderness in northern Maine.)

- Sign me up.

- I wish I knew. I really do.

- It was at least three and a half meters long.

- Everything we do in life, we need to do it some way. And the way we do it gives us a certain experience. Enjoy that experience, learn from it, and grow.

- I miss you, Dad!

- I like running in the rain.

- Give me another Hefeweizen.

- Don't give me another Hefeweizen.

- When I have a rock in my shoe, I stop and take it out.

- I can't ... breathe.

- The equipment failed again.

- I'm not turning back now.

- Do you remember anything?

- I'll have another, super-sized. Yes, I'm sure.

- I did just get hit by lightning.

- I'll be all right.

- No, nothing's missing.

- Yeah, I know what I ordered. Please bring it.

- I'll be there in about three weeks.

- Hey, what are you doing?

- It ran after me.

- If I'm lying on the ground mumbling, I'm probably saying something like: "Give me a Dels."

- Sticks and stones, baby. Sticks and stones.

- Umm, hello!

- Yeah, I've been there before.

- I love you and miss you so much, Mom!

- Are you sure?

- You tell me then.

- I can't figure this thing out, but neither can anyone else.

- Yeah, another flat.

- Did you bring it?

- I know it's hard.

- Never again. Okay, maybe once more.

- She ate the last one? There are none left!?

- I finished. I'm finished.

- I'm going to do it anyway.

- I don't care.

- Leave that alone, please.

- We've been waiting in line for three hours now.

- No, I can't believe it. Uh, yes I can.

- She said we could take as much as we wanted.

- Did that guy just cut me?

- No, I'm not full.

- I think we can make it.

- He was on his hind legs.

- She gave us this to share.

- Thanks. Thanks a million!

- Roger that. I'm coming right over.

- I'm sorry to hear that, she was a wonderful woman.

- Give me the pliers. I can't run with this toenail dangling.

- What do you mean we're out of Advil?

- Is that the last Band-Aid?

- Go buy 100 bottles of Gatorade.

- I've got 72 granola bars in my pack.

- It must last. It has too.

- I won.

- I didn't win.

- I finished. Thank, God. I didn't want to have to come back here.

- You're not from around here? Where are you from?

- Yes, I've eaten that before, but never again.

- My life wouldn't be complete without you.

- Thanks for everything that you've done for me. You've been wonderful.

- Yes, it means that much to me.

- No, I'm not going to do it that way.

- Go back, I think we missed it.

- I owe you an enormous debt of gratitude.

- Keep your eyes open, there's a big animal on the trail ahead of you.

- Yeah, I'm afraid. No, I'm not stopping.

- Let's hope we get better weather.

- Your hair is standing straight up.

- Glad we brought all this duct tape.

- Your nose is white. Cover it up.

- The guy's nose broke off, and that other guy, he lost an eye. I almost told him to look out the window.

- The pump broke.

- All I can promise you is that I'll give you one-hundred percent.

- I'm running out of cash.

- Can you wiggle your toes?

- What's the point? What's the point of anything?

- I can't see.

- I value my freedom. It's important to me.

- Count me in.

- I think we went into that corner too hot.

- Where were you going in such a hurry?

- It's definitely broken.

16. Frequently Asked Questions

"I paid already."

In this chapter I include a sampling of questions that I typically get asked, as well as my usual responses. The context is people whom I met on the road.

- How many times have you been struck by lightning?

  One time. It happened when I was hiking the AT. I've had many close calls.

- Didn't I see you about 50 miles ago?

  Yeah, probably.

- Are you tired?

  Yes, I'm exhausted.

- Ever get leeches?

  After a rain I once had 22 leeches on a run in Thailand. I'm glad I wasn't walking.

- How do you stay motivated?

It helps to have a specific goal. I usually set one or two major goals per year. I write them down. I focus on them.

- Why does a 60-year old man ride 100 miles on a bicycle?

I'm assuming this isn't a riddle. This man does it because he enjoys it.

- Have you encountered bears?

Yes, probably about 25. The closest encounter was on the CDT. I used my food bag as a pillow. In the Gila Wilderness, a black bear sniffing it woke me up. My tent siding was mesh. I saw his nose 12 inches from my face. Fortunately, when I screamed a series of expletives, he scampered away.

- Have you had any close calls?

Yes. Many. I feel fortunate to be alive. Many close calls were related to Mother Nature. Others were near misses with vehicles on the road, while cycling. Numerous instances were when I lost control of my bicycle. Other times when I fell, while climbing.

- Are you traveling alone?

Yes.

- Do you need a place to stay tonight?

Yes.

- What's the hardest thing you've ever done?

In athletic terms it would be setting the FKT for the PCT. I pushed through tough conditions on a schedule. I took risks.

- Are you scared?

Yes.

- How do you get through a bad patch in a race? Or, through a long day?

The better prepared you are to take on a challenge, the easier it'll be to succeed. If you're in over your head, you'll need to back off. Take time to regroup. Try not to dwell on pain. Be realistic. Don't lie to yourself. Evaluate your situation and problem solve. You can try to distract yourself and that might work for a while, but eventually, you'll need to come to terms with reality. If you can make steady progress, that's important. Just keep working away at it.

- Are you hungry?

Yeah, I'm starving.

- Don't you have bad days?

Yeah, but the good far outnumber the bad. Just like people.

- Isn't it hard to remain disciplined and focused on your training? You've been training for over 50 years.

After doing a workout, I almost always feel better. Sometimes it's hard to start, but once I get going, I surprise myself. I usually feel good. The tough part is starting. On some days I have to force myself to get moving. Once I do, I'm glad I did. I try not to think about getting started and just get out there and get going.

- Would you like to race RAAM again?

Yes, if someone else pays for it. Actually, when you finance the entire undertaking yourself, it's very rewarding. I would like to ride RAW—the Race across the West.

- Are you ever going to do that again?

I doubt it.

- Do you have any regrets?

Yes, but I try not to dwell on them. I look to the future.

- Would you like a refill?

Yes.

- Ever been bitten by a snake?

No, but on the PCT, a rattler once struck my trekking pole. I've had many near misses. I was bitten by a black-widow spider in Italy. I got typhoid from a tick bite in Thailand.

- Do you think you could have made a living as a professional athlete?

In my prime in most sports, you couldn't make a decent living. With the salaries now, I would have pursued an athletic career. I love to train. I love to travel to events and compete. At a young age, I would have needed proper coaching and guidance.

I think that I had enough ability, will-power, discipline, competitiveness, and energy to make it in some sports. In other sports my physical limitations would have prevented me from competing at the professional level. Although I loved basketball, I never could have played in the NBA. There are few players who are 5' 10" that have made it. I wouldn't have been able to compete successfully against (great) athletes who doped.

- Have you ever been injured?

Yes. While cycling I broke my collarbone, when a motorcycle hit me. I've had many overuse injuries—patella tendonitis, inflamed iliotibial band, shin splints, stress fractures, piriformis-muscle issues, and plantar fasciitis. Other injuries include the following: dislocated thumb, sprained ankles, torn rotator cuff, and bone chips in my elbows. I tore something in my ankle. I've had eye problems. During my thru-hikes, I suffered a number of injuries. In general I remained remarkably healthy. With age I listen to my body better, and I'm getting injured less frequently.

- Why do you want to do that?

I don't know. I just do. I never thought about why.

- Are you planning to climb Mount Everest?

Maybe. It's still on the table.

- Do you honestly believe that you could have run a marathon on any given day during the last 40 years?

Yeah, with the exception of one or two days, when I was very sick.

- Will you keep competing?

  As long as I enjoy it, yes.

- Can I buy you a beer?

  Sure. I'll get the next round.

- What's the most ticks you ever had at one time?

  On the CDT in Wyoming, I once took off 12 ticks. I was worried about Rocky Mountain spotted fever.

- What's your favorite food?

  Alaskan King-Crab legs.

- What is your favorite race to compete in?

  The Boston Marathon. For that reason I completed it 10 times. I've never done any other race that many times.

- Ever fallen out of a raft or canoe?

  I capsized in a canoe. My friend and I were okay. I was never knocked out of a raft.

- What scares you the most?

  Bad people.

- Don't you get bored while training?

No, never. I enjoy the process. There's much to think about in life. While I'm training, I do my thinking. I monitor my body. I enjoy being out in nature and looking at my surroundings.

- You're thin. Why are you running?

I enjoy running.

- Are you afraid of sharks?

When diving, no. I have a healthy respect for them.

- Don't your knees hurt?

Generally, no. I have no knee pain. If my knees get sore, I ice them. In RAAM I spent a lot of time icing.

- Do you ever sing while out training?

When I'm hiking, I do. I know the lyrics to many songs and tinkered with the guitar. Fish wanted to call me Jukebox instead of Wall. While cycling in remote areas, I sometimes put in an earbud and listen to music with one ear. Once in a while, I get a song in my head while training, but I don't sing out loud. I play it mentally.

- What's your resting pulse?

For most of my adult life, it's been in the low 40s.

- What's your favorite sport to watch?

I love cycling. My favorite race is the Tour of Flanders (Ronde van Vlaanderen). I enjoy watching track and field (athletics).

- Any advice for young people?

Try the following for people of any age:

1. Get out and see the world.
2. Learn about other people and cultures.
3. Experience things firsthand.
4. Dispel myths.
5. Don't spend too much time on your mobile.
6. Keep your head up.
7. Observe your surroundings, while engaging your senses.
8. Learn the right way to do things, not the easy way.
9. Do things the right way.
10. Maintain integrity.
11. Invest in yourself.
12. Make good friends.
13. Help others who are less fortunate.
14. Be courteous and kind.
15. Think about others.
16. Be humble.
17. Set ambitious goals.
18. Pretend you're a student and keep learning.
19. Don't be afraid to take chances, but don't expect results without preparation.
20. Strive for improvement.
21. Understand process is important to the end result.
22. Let those you love know it.
23. Compliment people, when they deserve it.
24. Don't be afraid to show emotion.
25. Admit when you're wrong.
26. Don't be afraid to lose face.
27. Cry when you feel like it.
28. Formulate and follow your dreams.
29. Plan, but don't over plan.
30. Be flexible.

31. Do your own research.
32. Be willing to compromise, but don't compromise your values.
33. Admit you don't have all the answers.
34. Make a contribution to society and humanity.
35. Listen, learn, live, and love.
36. Unless asked, don't offer an opinion until you understand and are knowledgeable about a situation.
37. Don't be quick to judge.

17. Personal Proverbs

"I consider myself a student of the game, every game."

In this chapter I share some lessons that I learned. I do this via short phrases. They relate to sports but can be applied to life in general.

- There are no shortcuts on the road to personal development.

- When the going gets tough, it helps to have practical experience.

- There are things that you can't do or achieve, and you must come to terms with this fact.

- You must accept reality, to deny it, is to lie to yourself.

- The things I remember are the people and the experiences, not the details.

- Each day we have choices. We must consider those choices and consciously select our best course of action.

- Planning is important, but flexibility is more important.

- You must develop your problem-solving skills in order to be able to solve your problems.

- You must develop your inner strength to the point where your values and convictions don't waiver.

- Belief without proper preparation can shatter your confidence.

- Through repetition and hard work, you must earn your own confidence.

- Not every day can be a good day, but one good day negates many bad days.

- You must accept and respect yourself in order for others to do the same.

- There are times when you should follow the wind, and others, when you need to alter your course. You need to be able to differentiate between the two.

- Time is fleeting, but greatness is permanent.

- Curiosity is something we need in order to survive.

- Focus on the variables that you can control, to clutter your mind with other things is an unproductive use of energy.

- Many things in the world are arbitrary but don't take them for granted.

- Using your best judgment make a decision, follow through. If you were wrong, admit it, and make adjustments.

- A small act of kindness is all that is needed to improve someone's day. Go ahead and make someone's day.

- Winning is important, but competing fairly is more important.

- When an individual strives for excellence in any pursuit, humanity benefits.

- To move from caves to populating the Earth, someone had to be curious; someone had to take the first step.

- Don't try to bend the rules. If the shoe doesn't fit, don't wear it.

- Your actions define you.

- A smile and a few kind words can diffuse many tense situations.

- To share an activity with a friend adds meaning to every human endeavor.

- The process involved in achieving athletic excellence is the process involved in achieving any excellence.

- To admit defeat requires greater courage than to acknowledge a victory.

- A positive attitude goes a long way to living a happy life.

18. Pet Peeves

"He did just bite me."

In this chapter I list my pet peeves. Some are meant in jest. Some are outside the realm of sports.

- Inconsiderate people.

- Dogs that bite.

- People who cut in line.

- People who don't take care of their pets.

- Negative people.

- People who comment on what other people are doing. Noisy people.

- People who have never done anything and have no experience yet provide their expert advice and critique.

- People who say any of the following:

    - Don't do that.
    - You're crazy.
    - You look tired.
    - That's dangerous.

- That's impossible.
- I don't believe you.
- How old are you?
- Where did you come from?
- Need a ride?
- Do you want to give up?
- You don't look too good.
- It's all downhill from here.

- People who return a car with an empty gas tank.

- People who throw empty beer bottles at you.

- People who eat the last bag of chips.

- People and countries who don't learn from their mistakes.

- People who complain about everything.

- People who don't accept reality.

- People who say they are sorry, when they aren't.

- Nearby smokers.

- Drivers who run cyclists off the road.

- People who work in the service industry but are preoccupied with a mobile device, which isn't being used to service you.

- People who live exclusively in the virtual world.

- Critics with no experience, accomplishments, or credentials.

- People who don't clean up after their pets.

- People who break promises.

- People who lie.

- Shoes or clothes that don't run true to size.

- Flat tires.

- People who bump into you, while staring at their mobiles.

- People who talk loudly on mobiles in public spaces.

- Close-minded people.

- People who don't accept people for whom they are.

- Backpackers who take breaks in the middle of a trail.

- People who try to convert you to their religion.

- People who don't respect others.

- People who invade your space.

- Political advertisements that block sidewalks or aren't removed after elections.

- Litter.

- Terrible smells.

- People who use their hazard lights to give themselves a license to park anywhere.

- People who waste food.

- People who steal or cheat.

- People who beat around the bush.

- People who exploit others.

- People who make false claims.

- People who swear at you or give you the middle finger.

- People who don't apologize.

- Divers who break coral or touch sea life.

- Aggressive salespeople.

- People who ask to borrow your money even though they're better off financially.

- Parents who ignore their children.

- Teachers who don't teach.

- Wasted food.

- People who shirk their responsibilities.

- Pork-barrel legislation.

- People who want to be friends, but for the wrong reasons.

- People who don't dispose of chewing gum properly.

- Birds who poop on your head.

- Self-serving oligarchies.

- Unnecessary or totally meaningless requirements and/or paperwork.

- Restaurant servers who don't pay attention.

- People who blame others for their own mistakes.

19. Personal Philosophy

"Less is more, more or less."

In this chapter I share one liners about my philosophy. My mother was a great one for pithy sayings. I don't claim that all these are original. I have no citations though. These include principles that I try to follow. These piggyback on my personal proverbs.

- Leave no footprints.

- Reduce clutter in life by simplifying and resisting the desire to possess material things.

- Be true to oneself.

- Don't try to impress people.

- Create your own dreams and follow them.

- Accept help from others.

- Offer your assistance to others, especially those less fortunate.

- Be thankful for what you have.

- Live and let live.

- Respect all life.

- Treat all human beings equally and with respect.

- Enjoy each day and consider tomorrow a bonus.

- Make flexible plans.

- Remember there's always someone else far worse off than you.

- Share with others.

- Be kind to yourself and others.

- Realize that not everyone is as fortunate or healthy as you.

- Understand your fears and limitations.

- Don't focus on negatives or dwell on problems.

- Enjoy your successes and take time to smell the roses.

- When you get knocked down, learn from your mistakes and get back up.

- Dream.

- When you feel your energy is ebbing, eat or drink something.

- If you have a problem, solve it. Or, reach out to someone who can help you solve it.

- Things don't get better on their own.

- It's important to find a balance in life, and what is in balance today may be out of balance tomorrow.

- Don't dwell on bad luck or misfortune, or aches and pains.

- When you start to think about retirement often, it means you've waited too long.

- It's wise not to delay activities for they may never be available again.

- It's more enjoyable to do something than to think about doing something.

20. Personal Mantras

"Repeat after me."

In this chapter I list a number of phrases that I repeat to help get me through difficult times. Sometimes it's not the words themselves that are important but simply engaging the mind in a repetitive process. Remember to start the process before it becomes too late. A few deep breaths help. At times just looking around at your surroundings can provide relief, as can a momentary pause. A micro-rest may be all that is needed.

- You can do this.

- Come on, keep going.

- This too will pass.

- You're almost there.

- You're strong. Don't give in.

- Looking good.

- This will be over soon.

- You've got this.

- This is easy.

- You've been here before.

- A few more days and you're done.

- One more time.

- You need to keep moving.

- Go, go, go.

- Keep working away at it.

- There's nothing to fear but fear itself.

- You've done your homework.

- You're not safe here.

- Just ten more steps.

- There's nothing that you can do about that.

- Concentrate on what you're capable of doing.

- Have patience.

- Slowly, slowly.

- Failure isn't an option.

- Put one foot in front of the other.

- It's too bad this is almost over.

- Stay focused.

- You're making good progress.

- Don't give in; don't give up.

- You're Raymond Greenlaw.

21. What's Next?

"What have you done lately?"

I list some future plans. Staying fit has allowed me to pursue many non-athletic goals. My book *Raymond's Checklist for His Personal Bucket List* contains an extensive list of things that I want to do. As of this writing, COVID-19 has restricted travel throughout the world. During lockdowns, I wasn't able to train to the extent desired. The list presented here is driven by the pandemic. In the near term, I scaled back my ambitions.

- Live and train in Africa for one year.

- Dive Ningaloo Reef.

- Dive in the Solomon Islands.

- Complete another thru-hike of the CDT.

- Walk across Mongolia.

- Ride the Race across the West.

- Compete in a half Ironman.

- Help others achieve their goals.

- Bring my life-time marathon per year average back up to one.

- Run some half marathons.

- Complete a bike ride from Alaska to Patagonia.

- Follow the Vuelta a España for three weeks around Spain.

- Hike the Haute Route Pyrenees from the Mediterranean Sea to the Atlantic Ocean.

- Compete in marathon swims.

- Ride across Thailand via the hard mountainous route.

- Get together with my family and friends and share in fun outdoor activities.

22. Summary

"You get what you give."

My original goal in writing this book was to produce my palmarès. I figured this task would help shape my future plans. It has done that. I can see where I spent my time over the past years and where I would like to direct future efforts. This process gave me time to reflect. I learned what activities impacted my life the most, helped me grow, and were enjoyable. I discovered what things I remember, how well I remember them, and the ones I remember in a favorable way. Through the experiences in my palmarès, I built a lot of memories. I draw on those in daily life.

We can't redo the past but through a process of review and reflection, we can decide how best to move forward. I spent much of my free time training and preparing for the activities in my palmarès. I trained with friends and that process built my strongest bonds. I also trained alone, which helped strengthen me. Time spent training gave me time for reflection and deep thought. I learned my mental and physical limits. Knowing these boundaries helped me extend them and at other times alerted me to needing to back down.

I can't help but think of the number of days that I spent having sore legs. Whenever I pushed myself hard in a marathon, ultra-marathon, or Ironman, I was sore for two to five days. And in some cases, if I made an extreme effort, I wouldn't recover for weeks. With the longevity of my athletic career, I spent at least 1,000 days with a sore and fatigued body—unable to walk up and down stairs properly. Sometimes I laughed at how much I hurt or how sore I was, but those days weren't fun. They forced down time.

In RAAM I did permanent nerve damage to my feet and hands. After my two solo efforts, I pedaled in bed for about seven weeks. I worried I needed to ride, that I was behind schedule. The preparation time, my nerve damage, the sacrifices, the suffering, the months recovering, and the financial burden were offset by the positives of bonding with crew members, self-discovery, camaraderie with other racers, memories added, and personal growth.

I'm glad I rode RAAM. I think of my crew members often, and the hardships they endured on my behalf. Their willingness to support me has given great meaning to my life. The human bonding developed through sharing a difficult experience is etched in our DNA. I'm glad I participated in the other activities described in my palmarès. Extreme endurance sports are a re-creation of our ancestors' struggle for survival. Striving is part of human essence. Without taking on challenges, without helping one another, and without the collective, the human race wouldn't survive.

When I think of the greatest palmarès of all-time, I think of the cyclist Eddy "The Cannibal" Merckx. Depending on your source, he won 525 out of 1,600 races in an 18-year career (amateur and pro), including 11 grand tours, all five cycling monuments at least twice, and three world championships. He won all important bike races at least once and set the hour record. Merckx never won a gold medal, as professional athletes were banned from the Olympics until 1986. He raced from 1961-78. The Cannibal won three times as many races as I entered.

In every sport there are exceptional palmarès. When people discuss the greatest athletes of all-time, a wide variety of sports and names are bantered about. I remember Jim Thorpe's name from my childhood. He won both the pentathlon and decathlon in the 1912 Olympics. The Native American played professional baseball, basketball, and football. I can't imagine someone playing MLB, in the NBA, and the NFL and also winning gold medals in the pentathlon and decathlon in modern times. I don't think anyone else can imagine it either. Thorpe was a magnificent athlete and a remarkable inspiration.

The accomplishments of the greatest champions are mind boggling. They inspire me. I won almost no races. I'm not a professional athlete. I pursued a number of different sports to share experiences with friends, to enrich my life, to learn more about myself, and to dream I was on the big stage with the greats. I was lucky to compete head-to-head against some of the best ever in many sports. I found strength and courage in the amazing feats of others.

This book is a tribute to those who devoted themselves to their chosen endeavors and followed a challenging path. The value of their inspirations and contributions to humanity are immeasurable. We can't all be champions. In a competition there's only one winner. But if we each push ourselves in the right direction, we can become a better civilization. We can and should strive to inspire the next generation. In a time of wide-spread unrest and uncertainty, athletes striving to achieve excellence become important role models and leaders. I admire those who shoulder that burden well. I find that the same qualities that lead to success in sport lead to success in life.

Appendix A:
Fastest Known Time Guidelines

"It's good to see you pushing the envelope."

In this appendix I present guidelines for record-setting considerations for the fastest hike of a trail. Records for fastest hikes are commonly referred to as *Fastest Known Times* (FKTs). These guidelines (Raymond's Guidelines for Setting a Fastest Known Time) are intended so that the following statements hold:

1. A performance can be (easily) understood and quantified.
2. A level playing field with fair rules is available to any challenger of a record.
3. Performances can be compared and evaluated.
4. The integrity of a performance is ensured.
5. Records are meaningful.
6. If the guidelines are followed and the existing record is broken, everyone will agree that the new time is the new record.

In my book *Raymond's Checklist for Gear for a Long Hike*, I present these guidelines with an expanded discussion. My guidelines are directed toward well-marked trails such as the Appalachian (AT) and Pacific Crest Trails (PCT), where record-breaking attempts have become popular even at the international level. I frame my recommendations so they apply to any trail.

Because my guidelines apply equally well to venues other than trails (roads, waterways, and so forth), I use the word *course* in my discussion. A course starts at point S (the *start*) and finishes at point F (the *finish line* or *terminus*). For a loop course, S and T are the same. These guidelines don't specifically address non-continuous or segmented courses. In extending them to such courses, the main issues are direction of travel, means of transportation allowed between segments, order of completion, and whether individual segments must be completed fully in one go.

When a course isn't well defined, a FKT doesn't make sense, unless the goal is simply to get from S to T via any route. In this case a FKT isn't set for a particular course but rather for going between two points. Once a route is fixed, a FKT can be discussed for that course. For example, there could be a FKT for the Bear Creek Route of the Continental Divide Trail (CDT). We can talk about a FKT from the US-Mexican border at Puerto Palomas, New Mexico to the CDT monument on the US-Canadian border between Waterton Lakes National Park, Alberta and Glacier National Park, Montana via any route, including road walking. Without qualifiers or course specification, talking about a FKT for the CDT doesn't make sense though because for CDT thru-hikers there are many options. The actual method of progression along a course and other factors are important, too.

I take the following statement to be self-evident:

If an athlete doesn't complete a course in its entirety, the athlete can't break the course record.

While keeping my original goals in mind, statements 1–6 presented earlier, I came up with a set of guidelines. I pared them down to the minimal set of rules that allows statements 1–6 to be satisfied. If I thought a point wasn't self-evident (to all), I added a rule for it. If adhered to, my guidelines are sufficient to guarantee a best time for a course is record worthy. If a challenger states: "I adhered to Raymond's Guidelines for Setting a Fastest Known Time," no one will question whether the performance is record worthy. For more lenient sets of guidelines, not everyone will agree that a record has been set. This situation can lead to confusion.

As noted, a more thorough presentation of these guidelines is given in my book *Raymond's Checklist for Gear for a Long Hike*. It's worth reading that discussion to see why some rules are important and required. For participants not interested in FKTs, simply enjoy your journey in any manner that you please. For those interested in FKTs, I suggest you follow a set of rules that respects the process and those who came before you. In such cases maintaining integrity is the key to having a meaningful FKT.

Note that in my guidelines I use ST (FT) to represent the actual starting (respectively, finishing) time. So for example, ST might be May 11, 2003 at 11:15:23 AM PT. My recommendations follow. Discussion continues after the guidelines.

Raymond's Guidelines for Setting a Fastest Known Time (FKT)

1. <u>Progression:</u> All forward progress must be made through one's own locomotion, either on foot or by crawling.

2. <u>Recovery:</u> If an athlete veers off course or gets lost, the athlete must resume forward progress from the point of deviation.

3. <u>Timing:</u> The elapsed time (FT – ST) from the starting time (ST) at the course's beginning until the finishing time (FT) at the end is the time taken to complete the course.

4. <u>Performance Enhancement:</u> Prior to ST, the athlete must adhere to the World Anti-Doping Agency's (WADA) rules. Once the journey begins, WADA's rules in effect at ST must be met until FT.

5. <u>Record Holder:</u> The record holder for the FKT is the athlete who completes the entire course in a continuous, single-direction traverse in the least amount of time, while complying with these guidelines from ST until FT.

6. <u>Completeness:</u> No set of guidelines can address every possible situation. Integrity, sportsmanship, and faithfulness to the course must be maintained in the spirit of these guidelines to address situations that aren't specifically covered.

While adhering to these guidelines, it's not possible to set a record for some courses at a particular time of year or perhaps even at any time in some years. That is to say due to extenuating circumstances, it might not be possible to complete a course in its entirety. Sections of a course may be closed for a plethora of reasons. In such years some performances may be noteworthy. They can be footnoted and given an honorable mention.

A FKT applies to a particular, specific course. Consider the AT. It doesn't make sense to talk about a FKT for a course "equivalent" to the AT being used to set the FKT on the AT. To set the FKT on the AT, one must complete the AT. This point should be clear. Note that the AT itself does contain white blazed high- and low-water routes. Any official part of the route suffices. Rules 5 and 6 are applicable here.

Note that some courses may recognize specialized or restricted records, for example, the fastest crossing in winter. The general guidelines presented can be extended to these situations. For example, for winter records in the northern hemisphere, we can specify that the starting and finishing times are in the interval from December 21 at 12:00 AM EST until March 20 at 12:00 PM EST. Another possibility is a fixed direction, for example, the FKT for a north-to-south versus a south-to-north traverse. The Comrades Marathon is one well-known course that maintains both 'up' and 'down' FKTs. As of this writing, the men's records differ by six minutes and thirty seconds, whereas the women's by four minutes and ten seconds. In both cases the down records (Pietermaritzburg to Durban) are faster.

When FKT rules become overly complex, it indicates that the spirit of an activity has been lost. The competition is no longer sporting, and records become meaningless. Tarman and I joked that he bagged the FKT for an over-65 male with a total-ankle replacement to section hike the then-open PCT over a period of five non-consecutive years. Then we got into the details about what constitutes a total-ankle replacement, exactly when he turned 65, what sections were considered officially open, and so forth. An athlete can set a FKT for a course that they dream up or for a reasonable alternative to a known course, and with enough qualifiers and modifiers, everyone can be a record holder, but such an athlete isn't setting the record for a known, repeatable course such as the AT or PCT.

One should recognize that many hikers don't support record-setting attempts or aren't interested in such activities. While engaging in a record attempt, it helps to be mindful of this fact and to treat others courteously. Hike your own hike. If you want to set a FKT follow well-established guidelines and fair rules and don't compromise your own integrity and credibility. If less stringent guidelines than these are followed, someone might not agree that a record was broken.

In the interest of these guidelines evolving, unlike other parts of this book which are bound by copyright, Roxy Publishing gives readers permission to republish these guidelines in part or in whole with a proper citation to this book. For those following these guidelines and wanting to establish that their record was set under fair conditions, they may state: "My time was set while adhering to Raymond's Guidelines for Setting a FKT." In such cases I don't think there can be any debate about whether a new record was established fairly.

Books By Raymond Greenlaw

PALMARÈS (also available in electronic form).

The Thai Wife Story JOY (also available in electronic form), Book 1 of *The Thai Wife Series of Novels*.

The Thai Wife Story STAR (also available in electronic form), Book 2 of *The Thai Wife Series of Novels*.

Raymond's Checklist for Traveling in the USA (also available in electronic form), Book 1 of *Raymond's Checklist Series*.

Raymond's Checklist for Traveling in Thailand (also available in electronic form), Book 2 of *Raymond's Checklist Series*.

Raymond's Checklist for Traveling the World (also available in electronic form), Book 3 of *Raymond's Checklist Series*.

Raymond's Checklist for His Personal Bucket List (also available in electronic form), Book 4 of *Raymond's Checklist Series*.

Raymond's Checklist for Gear for a Long Hike (also available in electronic form), Book 5 of *Raymond's Checklist Series*.

Raymond's Checklist Cycling Gear (also available in electronic form), Book 6 of *Raymond's Checklist Series*.

The Hazards of Cycling in Thailand: Guidelines for Tourists (also available in electronic form).

Trapped in Thailand's Cave (also available in electronic form).

The Pacific Crest Trail: Its Fastest Hike, second edition (also available in electronic form).

Bob: My Dad, the Fisherman: A Father and Son's Relationship (also available in electronic form).

(With Saowaluk Rattanaudomsawat) *Essential Conversational Thai: Learn to Speak Thai Quickly, while Traveling in Thailand.*

You'll Never Walk Alone: Love Poems for My Sweetheart (also available in electronic form).

Poems of Raymond Greenlaw, 1986–2005 (also available in electronic form).

The Fastest Hike across Thailand (expected December 2021).

ABOUT THE AUTHOR

Raymond "Wall" Greenlaw was born in Providence, Rhode Island, USA to Roxy and Bob. Raymond has always enjoyed nature, big trees, lakes, mountains, and the sea. He writes about a wide range of topics and is the author of 35+ books.

www.ingramcontent.com/pod-product-compliance
Lightning Source LLC
LaVergne TN
LVHW051044080426
835508LV00019B/1703